| | DATE DUE | | |
|---|---|---|---|
| | | | |
| | | | |
| | | | |
| | | | |
| | | | |
| | | | |
| | | | |
| | | | |
| | | | |
| | | | |
| | | | |
| | | | |

# A REVISION OF THE TREATY

*The Collected Writings of John Maynard Keynes*

# THE COLLECTED WRITINGS OF
# JOHN MAYNARD KEYNES

VOLUME III

# A REVISION OF THE TREATY

BEING A SEQUEL TO
*THE ECONOMIC CONSEQUENCES
OF THE PEACE*

MACMILLAN
ST MARTIN'S PRESS
FOR THE
ROYAL ECONOMIC SOCIETY

First edition 1922
Reprinted 1922
This edition 1971

· Published by
THE MACMILLAN PRESS LTD
London and Basingstoke
Associated companies in New York Toronto
Dublin Melbourne Johannesburg and Madras

SBN 333 10718 7

Library of Congress catalog card no. 76–133449

Printed in Great Britain
at the University Printing House, Cambridge
(Brooke Crutchley, University Printer)

# CONTENTS

v

APPENDIX OF DOCUMENTS

# GENERAL INTRODUCTION

This new standard edition of *The Collected Writings of John Maynard Keynes* forms the memorial to him of the Royal Economic Society. He devoted a very large share of his busy life to the Society. In 1911, at the age of twenty-eight, he became editor of the *Economic Journal* in succession to Edgeworth; two years later he was made secretary as well. He held these offices without intermittence until almost the end of his life. Edgeworth, it is true, returned to help him with the editorship from 1919 to 1925; MacGregor took Edgeworth's place until 1934, when Austin Robinson succeeded him and continued to assist Keynes down to 1945. But through all these years Keynes himself carried the major responsibility and made the principal decisions about the articles that were to appear in the *Economic Journal*, without any break save for one or two issues when he was seriously ill in 1937. It was only a few months before his death at Easter 1946 that he was elected president and handed over his editorship to Roy Harrod and the secretaryship to Austin Robinson.

In his dual capacity of editor and secretary Keynes played a major part in framing the policies of the Royal Economic Society. It was very largely due to him that some of the major publishing activities of the Society—Sraffa's edition of Ricardo, Stark's edition of the economic writings of Bentham, and Guillebaud's edition of Marshall, as well as a number of earlier publications in the 1930s—were initiated.

When Keynes died in 1946 it was natural that the Royal Economic Society should wish to commemorate him. It was perhaps equally natural that the Society chose to commemorate him by producing an edition of his collected works. Keynes himself had always taken a joy in fine printing, and the Society, with the help of Messrs Macmillan as publishers and the Cambridge University Press as printers, has been anxious to give Keynes's writings a permanent form that is wholly worthy of him.

The present edition will publish as much as is possible of his work in the field of economics. It will not include any private and personal correspondence or publish letters in the possession of his family. The edition is concerned, that is to say, with Keynes as an economist.

Keynes's writings fall into five broad categories. First there are the books which he wrote and published as books. Second there are collections of articles and pamphlets which he himself made during his lifetime (*Essays in Persuasion* and *Essays in Biography*). Third, there is a very considerable volume of published but uncollected writings—articles written for newspapers, letters to newspapers, articles in journals that have not been included in his two volumes of collections, and various pamphlets. Fourth, there are a few hitherto unpublished writings. Fifth, there is correspondence with economists and concerned with economics or public affairs.

This series will attempt to publish a complete record of Keynes's serious writing as an economist. It is the intention to publish almost completely the whole of the first four categories listed above. The only exceptions are a few syndicated articles where Keynes wrote almost the same material for publication in different newspapers or in different countries, with minor and unimportant variations. In these cases, this series will publish one only of the variations, choosing the most interesting.

The publication of Keynes's economic correspondence must inevitably be selective. In the day of the typewriter and the filing cabinet and particularly in the case of so active and busy a man, to publish every scrap of paper that he may have dictated about some unimportant or ephemeral matter is impossible. We are aiming to collect and publish as much as possible, however, of the correspondence in which Keynes developed his own ideas in argument with his fellow economists, as well as the more significant correspondence at times when Keynes was in the middle of public affairs.

Apart from his published books, the main sources available to those preparing this series have been two. First, Keynes in his will made Richard Kahn his executor and responsible for his economic papers. They have been placed in the Marshall Library of the University of Cambridge and have been available for this edition. Until 1914 Keynes did not have a secretary and his earliest papers are in the main limited to drafts of important letters that he made in his own handwriting and retained. At that stage most of the correspondence that we possess is represented by what he received rather than by what he wrote. During the war years of 1914–18 Keynes was serving in the Treasury. With the recent opening of the records under the thirty-year rule, many of the papers that he wrote then and later have become available. From 1919 onwards, throughout the rest of his life, Keynes had the help of a secretary—for many years Mrs Stevens. Thus for the last twenty-five years of his working life we have in most cases the carbon copies of his own letters as well as the originals of the letters that he received.

There were, of course, occasions during this period on which Keynes wrote himself in his own handwriting. In some of these cases, with the help of his correspondents, we have been able to collect the whole of both sides of some important interchange and we have been anxious, in justice to both correspondents, to see that both sides of the correspondence are published in full.

The second main source of information has been a group of scrapbooks kept over a very long period of years by Keynes's mother, Florence Keynes, wife of Neville Keynes. From 1919 onwards these scrapbooks contain almost the whole of Maynard Keynes's more ephemeral writing, his letters to newspapers and a great deal of material which enables one to see not only what he wrote, but the reaction of others to his writing. Without these very carefully kept scrapbooks the task of any editor or biographer of Keynes would have been immensely more difficult.

The plan of the edition, as at present intended, is this. It will total twenty-four volumes. Of these, the first eight will be Keynes's published books from *Indian Currency and Finance*, in

1913, to the *General Theory* in 1936, with the addition of his *Treatise on Probability*. There will next follow, as vols. IX and X, *Essays in Persuasion* and *Essays in Biography*, representing Keynes's own collections of articles. *Essays in Persuasion* will differ from the original printing in two respects; it will contain the full texts of the articles or pamphlets included in it and not (as in the original printing) abbreviated versions of these articles, and it will have added one or two later articles which are of exactly the same character as those included by Keynes in his original collection. In the case of *Essays in Biography*, we shall add one or two other biographical studies that Keynes wrote later than 1933.

There will follow three volumes, XI to XIV, of economic articles and correspondence, and one volume of social, political, and literary writings. We shall include in these volumes such part of Keynes's economic correspondence as is closely associated with the articles that are printed in them.

The further nine volumes, as we estimate at present, will deal with Keynes's *Activities* during the years from the beginning of his public life in 1905 until his death. In each of the periods into which we propose to divide this material, the volume concerned will publish his more ephemeral writings, all of it hitherto uncollected, his correspondence relating to these activities, and such other material and correspondence as is necessary to the understanding of Keynes's activities. These volumes are being edited by Elizabeth Johnson and Donald Moggridge, and it is their task to trace and interpret Keynes's activities sufficiently to make the material fully intelligible to a later generation. Until this work has progressed further, it is not possible to say with exactitude whether this material will be distributed, as we now think, over nine volumes, or whether it will need to be spread over a further volume or volumes. There will be a final volume of bibliography and index.

Those responsible for this edition have been: Lord Kahn, both as Lord Keynes's executor and as a long and intimate friend of

Lord Keynes, able to help in the interpreting of much that would otherwise be misunderstood; Sir Roy Harrod as the author of his biography; Austin Robinson as Keynes's co-editor on the *Economic Journal* and successor as secretary of the Royal Economic Society. The initial editorial tasks were carried by Elizabeth Johnson. More recently she has been joined in this responsibility by Donald Moggridge. They have been assisted at different times by Jane Thistlethwaite, Mrs McDonald, who was originally responsible for the systematic ordering of the files of the Keynes papers, Judith Masterman, who for many years worked with Mrs Johnson on the papers and more recently by Susan Wilsher and Margaret Butler.

# EDITORIAL FOREWORD

*A Revision of the Treaty* was largely the product of a period of discussion with Harcourt, Brace during the summer and autumn of 1921. In June 1921, Keynes had proposed to Alfred Harcourt that he prepare for publication at the end of 1921 'a final revised edition' of *The Economic Consequences of the Peace*. For this edition he proposed to write a new introduction of some 40 pages, to leave the present text as it stood and to deal with new facts or criticisms in footnotes or a series of appendices to the chapters of *Economic Consequences*.

To this proposal Alfred Harcourt replied in late June that Keynes 'give something near to prayerful consideration to making a new book out of the new material and even such old material...from "The Economic Consequences of the Peace"' as he needed. He strongly argued the case for a restatement, saying that the public would not buy or read a revision but merely take note of the changes from reviews, and that Keynes would write a better book freed from the constraints of the earlier work.

Keynes appears to have accepted this proposal with alacrity, for on 3 August he sent Harcourt a draft table of contents for a volume of about 40,000 words entitled 'Essays Supplementary to *The Economic Consequences of the Peace*'. This table, which is of interest, is printed below.

'Essays Supplementary to
*The Economic Consequences of the Peace*'

Preface
|  |  |  |
|---|---|---|
| I | Papers on the Economic Prospects 1921 | 20,000 words |
|  | (A) The Depreciation of Money |  |
|  | (B) Germany |  |
| II | The Reparation Bill | 6,000 words |
| III | Books on the Peace Conference | 5,000 words |
| IV | The Future of Europe | 8,000 words |
|  | Bibliographical Note on *The Economic Consequences of the Peace* | 1,000 words |

There matters stood until November. In the interim, Keynes had talked with Donald Brace, Alfred Harcourt's partner, in London and had heard of his dissatisfaction with the new title proposed by Keynes, 'German Reparation: Essays Supplementary to *The Economic Consequences of the Peace*'. On 2 November 1921 Keynes wrote Brace of his new proposal '*A Revision of the Treaty* being a sequel to *The Economic Consequences of the Peace*' and forwarded a revised table of contents which follows that finally printed except in one or two minor details.

*A Revision of the Treaty* was published in England in January 1922. As the first printing of 10,000 copies seemed likely to be quickly exhausted, it was reprinted in February 1922. The type was distributed in July 1922. By then 6,839 copies of the English edition had been sold. In the reprinted edition several minor corrections were made and a document on the Cannes Moratorium of January 1922 added. This edition follows the 1922 English reprint with one change, the removal of the excessive capitalisation followed by the printers of the day.

The book was separately printed and published for the American market by Messrs Harcourt, Brace. It was translated into French, German, Italian, Dutch, Swedish, Japanese and Russian. All of these translations carried in translation the standard English preface; unlike *The Economic Consequences of the Peace*, the French edition of *A Revision of the Treaty*, which, because a more literal translation seemed unacceptable to French readers, appeared under the title of *Nouvelles Considérations sur les Conséquences de la Paix*, had no special preface by Keynes himself; a short editorial foreword by the publishers is of no literary importance.

The Italian translation differs from the English reprint and all other editions with another two documents in the Appendix of Documents—an American note and a decision of the Reparations Commission of March 1922. Neither of these contains anything written by Keynes himself, and they have not been included in this volume.

# PREFACE

*The Economic Consequences of the Peace*, which I published in December 1919, has been reprinted from time to time without revision or correction. So much has come to our knowledge since then, that a revised edition of that book would be out of place. I have thought it better, therefore, to leave it unaltered, and to collect together in this *Sequel* the corrections and additions which the flow of events makes necessary, together with my reflections on the present facts.

But this book is strictly what it represents itself to be—a *Sequel*; I might almost have said an Appendix. I have nothing very new to say on the fundamental issues. Some of the remedies which I proposed two years ago are now everybody's commonplaces, and I have nothing startling to add to them. My object is a strictly limited one, namely, to provide facts and materials for an intelligent review of the reparation problem, as it now is.

'The great thing about this wood', said M. Clemenceau of his pine forest in La Vendée, 'is that here there is not the slightest chance of meeting Lloyd George or President Wilson. Nothing, here, but the squirrels.' I wish that I could claim the same advantages for this book.

J. M. KEYNES

*King's College, Cambridge*
*December 1921*

# Chapter 1

# THE STATE OF OPINION

It is the method of modern statesmen to talk as much folly as the public demand and to practise no more of it than is compatible with what they have said, trusting that such folly in action as must wait on folly in word will soon disclose itself as such, and furnish an opportunity for slipping back into wisdom—the Montessori system for the child, the public. He who contradicts this child will soon give place to other tutors. Praise, therefore, the beauty of the flames he wishes to touch, the music of the breaking toy; even urge him forward; yet waiting with vigilant care, the wise and kindly saviour of society, for the right moment to snatch him back, just singed and now attentive.

I can conceive for this terrifying statesmanship a plausible defence. Mr Lloyd George took the responsibility for a Treaty of Peace, which was not wise, which was partly impossible, and which endangered the life of Europe. He may defend himself by saying that he knew that it was not wise and was partly impossible and endangered the life of Europe; but that public passions and public ignorance play a part in the world of which he who aspires to lead a democracy must take account; that the Peace of Versailles was the best momentary settlement which the demands of the mob and the characters of the chief actors conjoined to permit; and for the life of Europe, that he has spent his skill and strength for two years in avoiding or moderating the dangers.

Such claims would be partly true and cannot be brushed away. The private history of the Peace Conference, as it has been disclosed by French and American participators, displays Mr Lloyd George in a partly favourable light, generally striving against the excesses of the Treaty and doing what he could, short of risking a personal defeat. The public history of the two years which have followed it exhibit him as protecting Europe from as many of the evil consequences of his own Treaty, as it lay in his power to prevent, with a craft few could have bettered, preserving the peace, though not the prosperity, of Europe, seldom expressing the truth, yet often acting under its influence. He would claim, therefore, that by devious paths, a faithful servant of the possible, he was serving man.

He may judge rightly that this is the best of which a democracy is capable—to be jockeyed, humbugged, cajoled along the right road. A preference for truth or for sincerity *as a method* may be a prejudice based on some aesthetic or personal standard, inconsistent, in politics, with practical good.

We cannot yet tell. Even the public learns by experience. Will the charm work still, when the stock of statesmen's credibility, accumulated before these times, is getting exhausted?

In any event, private individuals are not under the same obligation as cabinet ministers to sacrifice veracity to the public weal. It is a permitted self-indulgence for a private person to speak and write freely. Perhaps it may even contribute one ingredient to the congeries of things which the wands of statesmen cause to work together, so marvellously, for our ultimate good.

For these reasons I do not admit error in having based *The Economic Consequences of the Peace* on a literal interpretation of the Treaty of Versailles, or in having examined the results of actually carrying it out. I argued that much of it was *impossible*; but I do not agree with many critics, who held that for this very reason, it was also harmless. Inside opinion accepted from the beginning many of my main conclusions about the Treaty.[1] But it was not therefore unimportant that outside opinion should accept them also.

---

[1] 'Its merely colourable fulfilment of solemn contracts with a defeated nation, its timorous failure to reckon with economic realities', as Professor Allyn Young wrote in a review of my book. Yet Professor Young has thought right, nevertheless, to make himself a partial apologist of the Treaty, and to describe it as 'a forward-looking document'.

For there are, in the present times, two opinions; not, as in former ages, the true and the false, but the outside and the inside; the opinion of the public voiced by the politicians and the newspapers, and the opinion of the politicians, the journalists and the civil servants, upstairs and backstairs and behind-stairs, expressed in limited circles. In time of war it became a patriotic duty that the two opinions should be as different as possible; and some seem to think it so still.

This is not entirely new. But there has been a change. Some say that Mr Gladstone was a hypocrite; yet if so, he dropped no mask in private life. The high tragedians, who once ranted in the parliaments of the world, continued it at supper afterwards. But appearances can no longer be kept up behind the scenes. The paint of public life, if it is ruddy enough to cross the flaring footlights of today, cannot be worn in private—which makes a great difference to the psychology of the actors themselves. The multitude which lives in the auditorium of the world needs something larger than life and plainer than the truth. Sound itself travels too slowly in this vast theatre, and a true word no longer holds when its broken echoes have reached the farthest listener.

Those who live in the limited circles and share the inside opinion pay both too much and too little attention to the outside opinion; too much, because, ready in words and promises to concede to it everything, they regard open opposition as absurdly futile; too little, because they believe that these words and promises are so certainly destined to change in due season, that it is pedantic, tiresome, and inappropriate to analyse their literal meaning and exact consequences. They know all this nearly as well as the critic, who wastes, in their view, his time and his emotions in exciting himself too much over what, on his own showing, cannot possibly happen. Nevertheless, what is said before the world is, still, of deeper consequence than the subterranean breathings and well-informed whisperings, knowledge of which allows inside opinion to feel superior to outside opinion, even at the moment of bowing to it.

I-2

But there is a further complication. In England (and perhaps elsewhere also) there are *two* outside opinions, that which is expressed in the newspapers and that which the mass of ordinary men privately suspect to be true. These two degrees of the outside opinion are much nearer to one another than they are to the inside, and under some aspects they are identical; yet there is under the surface a real difference between the dogmatism and definiteness of the press and the living, indefinite belief of the individual man. I fancy that even in 1919 the average Englishman never really believed in the indemnity; he took it always with a grain of salt, with a measure of intellectual doubt. But it seemed to him that for the time being there could be little practical harm in going on the indemnity tack, and also that, in relation to his feelings at that time, a belief in the possibility of boundless payments by Germany was in better sentiment, even if less true, than the contrary. Thus the recent modification in British outside opinion is only partly intellectual, and is due rather to changed conditions; for it is seen that perseverance with the indemnity does now involve practical harm, whilst the claims of sentiment are no longer so decisive. He is therefore prepared to attend to arguments, of which he had always been aware out of the corner of his eye.

Foreign observers are apt to heed too little these unspoken sensibilities, which the voice of the press is bound to express ultimately. Inside opinion gradually affects them by percolating to wider and wider circles; and they are susceptible in time to argument, common sense, or self-interest. It is the business of the modern politician to be accurately aware of all three degrees; he must have enough intellect to understand the inside opinion, enough sympathy to detect the inner outside opinion, and enough brass to express the outer outside opinion.

Whether this account is true or fanciful, there can be no doubt as to the immense change in public sentiment over the past two years. The desire for a quiet life, for reduced commitments, for comfortable terms with our neighbours is now paramount. The megalomania of war has passed away, and every one wishes to conform himself with the facts. For these reasons the reparation chapter of the Treaty of Versailles is crumbling. There is little prospect now of the disastrous consequences of its fulfilment.

I undertake in the following chapters a double task, beginning with a chronicle of events and a statement of the present facts, and concluding with proposals of what we ought to do. I naturally attach primary importance to the latter. But it is not only of historical interest to glance at the recent past. If we look back a little closely on the two years which have just elapsed (and the general memory unaided is now so weak that we know the past little better than the future), we shall be chiefly struck, I think, by the large element of injurious make-believe. My concluding proposals assume that this element of make-believe has ceased to be politically necessary; that outside opinion is now ready for inside opinion to disclose, and act upon, its secret convictions; and that it is no longer an act of futile indiscretion to speak sensibly in public.

Chapter 2

# FROM THE RATIFICATION OF THE TREATY OF VERSAILLES TO THE SECOND ULTIMATUM OF LONDON

## I. THE EXECUTION OF THE TREATY AND THE PLEBISCITES

The Treaty of Versailles was ratified on 10 January 1920, and except in the plebiscite areas its territorial provisions came into force on that date. The Schleswig plebiscite (February and March 1920) awarded the north to Denmark and the south to Germany, in each case by a decisive majority. The East Prussian plebiscite (July 1920) showed an overwhelming vote for Germany. The Upper Silesian plebiscite (March 1921) yielded a majority of nearly two to one in favour of Germany for the province as a whole,[1] but a majority for Poland in certain areas of the south and east. On the basis of this vote, and having regard to the industrial unity of certain disputed areas, the principal Allies, with the exception of France, were of opinion that, apart from the south-eastern districts of Pless and Rybnik which, although they contain undeveloped coalfields of great importance, are at present agricultural in character, nearly the whole of the province should be assigned to Germany. Owing to the inability of France to accept this solution, the whole problem was referred to the League of Nations for final arbitration. This body bisected the industrial area in the interests of racial or national-

[1] More exactly, out of 1,220,000 entitled to vote and 1,186,000 actual voters, 707,000 votes or seven-elevenths were cast for Germany, and 479,000 votes or four-elevenths for Poland. Out of 1,522 communes, 844 showed a majority for Germany and 678 for Poland. The Polish voters were mainly rural, as is shown by the fact that in 36 towns Germany polled 267,000 votes against 70,000 for Poland, and in the country 440,000 votes against 409,000 for Poland.

istic justice; and introduced at the same time, in the endeavour to avoid the consequences of this bisection, complicated economic provisions of doubtful efficiency in the interests of material prosperity. They limited these provisions to fifteen years, trusting perhaps that something will have occurred to revise their decision before the end of that time. Broadly speaking, the frontier has been drawn, entirely irrespective of economic considerations, so as to include as large as possible a proportion of German voters on one side of it and Polish voters on the other (although to achieve this result it has been thought necessary to assign two almost purely German towns, Kattowitz and Konigshütte, to Poland). From this limited point of view the work may have been done fairly. But the Treaty had directed that economic and geographical considerations should be taken into account also.

I do not intend to examine in detail the wisdom of this decision. It is believed in Germany that subterranean influence brought to bear by France contributed to the result. I doubt if this was a material factor, except that the officials of the League were naturally anxious, in the interests of the League itself, to produce a solution which would not be a fiasco through the members of the Council of the League failing to agree about it amongst themselves; which inevitably imported a certain bias in favour of a solution acceptable to France. The decision raises, I think, much more fundamental doubts about this method of settling international affairs.

Difficulties do not arise in simple cases. The League of Nations will be called in where there is a conflict between opposed and incommensurable claims. A good decision can only result by impartial, disinterested, very well-informed and authoritative persons taking *everything* into account. Since international justice is dealing with vast organic units and not with a multitude of small units of which the individual particularities are best ignored and left to average themselves out, it cannot be the same thing as the cut-and-dried lawyer's justice of

7

the municipal court. It will be a dangerous practice, therefore, to entrust the settlement of the ancient conflicts now inherent in the tangled structure of Europe to elderly gentlemen from South America and the far Asiatic East, who will deem it their duty to extract a strict legal interpretation from the available signed documents—who will, that is to say, take account of as *few* things as possible, in an excusable search for a simplicity which is not there. That would only give us more judgements of Solomon with the ass's ears, a Solomon with the bandaged eyes of law who, when he says 'Divide ye the living child in twain', means it.

The Wilsonian dogma, which exalts and dignifies the divisions of race and nationality above the bonds of trade and culture, and guarantees frontiers but not happiness, is deeply embedded in the conception of the League of Nations as at present constituted. It yields us the paradox that the first experiment in international government should exert its influence in the direction of intensifying nationalism.

These parenthetic reflections have arisen from the fact that from a certain limited point of view the Council of the League may be able to advance a good case in favour of its decision. My criticism strikes more deeply than would a mere allegation of partiality.

With the conclusion of the plebiscites the frontiers of Germany were complete.

In January 1920 Holland was called on to surrender the Kaiser; and, to the scarcely concealed relief of the governments concerned, she duly refused (23 January 1920). In the same month the surrender of some thousands of 'war criminals' was claimed but, in the face of a passionate protest from Germany, was not insisted on. It was arranged instead that, in the first instance at least, only a limited number of cases should be pursued, not before Allied courts, as provided by the Treaty, but before the High Court of Leipzig. Some such cases have been tried; and now, by tacit consent, we hear no more about it.

On 13 March 1920, an outbreak by the reactionaries in Berlin

8

(the Kapp 'Putsch') resulted in their holding the capital for five days and in the flight of the Ebert government to Dresden. The defeat of this outbreak, largely by means of the weapon of the general strike (the first success of which was, it is curious to note, in defence of established order), was followed by Communist disturbances in Westphalia and the Ruhr. In dealing with this second outbreak, the German government despatched more troops into the district than was permissible under the Treaty, with the result that France seized the opportunity, without the concurrence of her Allies, of occupying Frankfurt (6 April 1920) and Darmstadt, this being the immediate occasion of the first of the series of allied conferences recorded below—the Conference of San Remo.

These events, and also doubts as to the capacity of the Central German government to enforce its authority in Bavaria, led to successive postponements of the completion of disarmament, due under the Treaty for 31 March 1920, until its final enforcement by the London Ultimatum of 5 May 1921.

There remains reparation, the chief subject of the chronicle which follows. In the course of 1920 Germany carried out certain specific deliveries and restitutions prescribed by the Treaty. A vast quantity of identifiable property, removed from France and Belgium, was duly restored to its owners.[1] The mercantile marine was surrendered. Some dyestuffs were delivered, and a certain quantity of coal. But Germany paid no cash, and the real problem of reparation was still postponed.[2]

With the conferences of the spring and summer of 1920 there began the long series of attempts to modify the impossibilities of the Treaty and to mould it into workable form.

---

[1] Up to 31 May 1920, securities and other identifiable assets to the value of 8,300 million francs and 500,000 tons of machinery and raw material had been restored to France (*Report of Finance Commission of French Chamber*, 14 June 1920), also 445,000 head of livestock.

[2] Up to May 1921, the *cash* receipts of the Reparation Commission amounted to no more than 124 million gold marks.

II. THE CONFERENCES OF SAN REMO (19–26 APRIL 1920), HYTHE (15 MAY AND 19 JUNE 1920), BOULOGNE (21–2 JUNE 1920), BRUSSELS (2–3 JULY 1920), AND SPA (5–16 JULY 1920)

It is difficult to keep distinct the series of a dozen discussions between the Premiers of the Allied Powers which occupied the year from April 1920 to April 1921. The result of each conference was generally abortive, but the total effect was cumulative; and by gradual stages the project of revising the Treaty gained ground in every quarter. The conferences furnish an extraordinary example of Mr Lloyd George's methods. At each of them he pushed the French as far as he could, but not as far as he wanted; and then came home to acclaim the settlement provisionally reached (and destined to be changed a month later) as an expression of complete accord between himself and his French colleague, as a nearly perfect embodiment of wisdom, and as a settlement which Germany would be well advised to accept as final, adding about every third time that, if she did not, he would support the invasion of her territory. As time went on, his reputation with the French was not improved; yet he steadily gained his object—though this may be ascribed not to the superiority of the method as such, but to facts being implacably on his side.

The first of the series, the Conference of San Remo (19–26 April 1920), was held under the presidency of the Italian Premier, Signor Nitti, who did not conceal his desire to revise the Treaty. M. Millerand stood, of course, for its integrity, whilst Mr Lloyd George (according to *The Times* of that date) occupied a middle position. Since it was evident that the French would not then accept any new formula, Mr Lloyd George concentrated his forces on arranging for a discussion face to face between the Supreme Council and the German government, such a meeting, extraordinary to relate, having never yet been arranged, neither during the Peace Conference nor afterwards. Defeated in a

proposal to invite German representatives to San Remo forthwith, he succeeded in carrying a decision to summon them to
visit Spa in the following month 'for the discussion of the
practical application of the Reparation Clauses'. This was the first
step; and for the rest the conference contented itself with a
Declaration on German Disarmament. Mr Lloyd George had
had to concede to M. Millerand that the integrity of the Treaty
should be maintained; but speaking in the House of Commons on
his return home, he admitted a preference for a not 'too literal'
interpretation of it.

In May the Premiers met in privacy at Hythe to consider their
course at Spa. The notion of the sliding scale, which was to play
a great part in the Paris Decisions and the Second Ultimatum of
London, now came definitely on the carpet. A committee of
experts was appointed to prepare for examination a scheme by
which Germany should pay a certain minimum sum each year,
supplemented by further sums in accordance with her capacity.
This opened the way for new ideas, but no agreement was yet in
sight as to actual figures. Meantime the Spa Conference was put
off for a month.

In the following month the Premiers met again at Boulogne
(21 June 1920), this meeting being preceded by an informal
weekend at Hythe (19 June 1920). It was reported that on this
occasion the Allies got so far as definitely to agree on the principle
of minimum annuities extensible in accordance with Germany's
economic revival. Definite figures even were mentioned, namely,
a period of thirty-five years and minimum annuities of three
milliard gold marks. The Spa Conference was again put off into
the next month.

At last the Spa meeting was really due. Again the Premiers met
(Brussels, 2–3 July 1920) to consider the course they would
adopt. They discussed many things, especially the proportions
in which the still hypothetical reparation receipts were to be
divided amongst the claimants.[1] But no concrete scheme was

---

[1] See Excursus 6.

adopted for reparation itself. Meanwhile a memorandum handed in by the German experts made it plain that no plan politically possible in France was economically possible in Germany. 'The Note of the German economic experts', wrote *The Times* on 3 July 1920, 'is tantamount to a demand for a complete revision of the Peace Treaty. The Allies have therefore to consider whether they will call the Germans sharply to order under the menace of definite sanctions, or whether they will risk creating the impression of feebleness by dallying with German tergiversations.' This was a good idea; if the Allies could not agree amongst themselves as to the precise way of altering the Treaty, a 'complete accord' between them could be re-established by 'calling the Germans sharply to order' for venturing to suggest that the Treaty could be altered at all.

At last, on 5 July 1920, the long-heralded Conference met. But, although it occupied twelve days, no time was found for reaching the item on the agenda which it had been primarily summoned to discuss—namely, reparations. Before this dangerous topic could be reached urgent engagements recalled M. Millerand to Paris. One of the chief subjects actually dealt with, coal, is treated in Excursus 1 at the conclusion of this chapter. But the chief significance of the meeting lay in the fact that then for the first time the responsible ministers and experts of Germany and the Allied states met face to face and used the methods of public conference and even private intimacy. The Spa Conference produced no plan; but it was the outward sign of some progress under the surface.

### III. THE BRUSSELS CONFERENCE (16–22 DECEMBER 1920)

Whilst the Spa Conference made no attempt to discuss the general question of the reparation settlement, it was again agreed that the latter should be tackled at an early date. But time passed by, and nothing happened. On 23 September 1920 M. Millerand succeeded to the Presidency of the French Republic, and his place as Premier was taken by M. Leygues. French official opinion steadily receded from the concessions, never fully admitted to the French public, which Mr Lloyd George had extracted at Boulogne. They now preferred to let the machinery of the Reparation Commission run its appointed course. At last, however, on 6 November 1920, after much diplomatic correspondence, it was announced that once again the French and British governments were in 'complete accord'. A conference of experts, nominated by the Reparation Commission, was to sit with German experts and report; then a conference of ministers was to meet the German government and report; with these two reports before it the Reparation Commission was to fix the amount of Germany's liability; and finally, the heads of the Allied governments were to meet and 'take decisions'. 'Thus,' *The Times* recorded, 'after long wanderings in the wilderness we are back once more at the Treaty of Versailles.' The re-perusal of old files of newspapers, which the industrious author has undertaken, corroborates, if nothing else does, the words of the Preacher and the dustiness of fate.

The first stage of this long procedure was in fact undertaken, and certain permanent officials of the Allied governments[1] met German representatives at Brussels, shortly before Christmas 1920, to ascertain facts and to explore the situation generally. This was a conference of 'experts' as distinguished from the conferences of 'statesmen' which preceded and followed it.

The work of the Brussels experts was so largely ignored and overthrown by the meetings of the statesmen at Paris shortly afterwards, that it is not now worth while to review it in detail. It marked, however, a new phase in our relations with Germany. The officials of the two sides met in an informal fashion and talked together like rational beings. They were representative of the pick of what might be called 'international officialdom',

[1] Lord D'Abernon and Sir John Bradbury for Great Britain, Seydoux and Cheysson for France, d'Amelio and Giannini for Italy, Delacroix and Lepreux for Belgium and, in accordance with custom, two Japanese. The German representatives included Bergmann, Havenstein, Cuno, Melchior, von Stauss, Bonn, and Schroeder.

cynical, humane, intelligent, with a strong bias towards facts and a realistic treatment. Both sides believed that progress was being made towards a solution; mutual respect was fostered; and a sincere regret was shared at the early abandonment of reasonable conversations.

The Brussels experts did not feel themselves free to consider an average payment less than that contemplated at Boulogne. They recommended to the Allied governments, accordingly:

(1) that during the five years from 1921 to 1926 Germany should pay an *average* annuity of £150 million (gold), but that this average annuity should be so spread over the five years that less than this amount would be payable in the first two years and more in the last two years, the question of the amount of subsequent payments, after the expiry of five years, being postponed for the present;

(2) that a substantial part of this sum should be paid in the form of deliveries of material and not of cash;

(3) that the annual expenses of the armies of occupation should be limited to £12 million (gold), which payment need not be additional to the above annuities but a first charge on them;

(4) that the Allies should waive their claim on Germany to build ships for them and should perhaps relinquish, or postpone, the claim for the delivery of a certain number of the existing German vessels;

(5) that Germany on her side should put her finances and her budget in order and should agree to the Allies taking control of her customs in the event of default under the above scheme.


IV. THE DECISIONS OF PARIS (24–30 JANUARY 1921)

The suggestions of the Brussels experts furnished no permanent settlement of the question, but they represented, nevertheless, a great advance from the ideas of the Treaty. In the meantime, however, opinion in France was rising against the concessions contemplated. M. Leygues, it appeared, would be unable to carry in the Chamber the scheme discussed at Boulogne. Prolonged political intrigue ended in the succession of M. Briand to the Premiership, with the extreme defenders of the literal integrity of the Treaty of Versailles, M. Poincaré, M. Tardieu, and M. Klotz, still in opposition. The projects of Boulogne and Brussels were thrown into the melting-pot, and another conference was summoned to meet at Paris at the end of January 1921.

It was at first doubtful whether the proceedings might not terminate with a breach between the British and the French points of view. Mr Lloyd George was justifiably incensed at having to surrender most of the ground which had seemed definitely gained at Boulogne; with these fluctuations negotiation was a waste of time and progress impossible. He was also disinclined to demand payments from Germany which *all* the experts now thought impossible. For a few days he was entirely unaccommodating to the French contentions; but as the business proceeded he became aware that M. Briand was a kindred spirit, and that, whatever nonsense he might talk in public, he was secretly quite sensible. A breach in the conversations might mean the fall of Briand and the entrance to office of the wild men, Poincaré and Tardieu who, if their utterances were to be taken seriously and were not merely a ruse to obtain office, might very well disturb the peace of Europe before they could be flung from authority. Was it not better that Mr Lloyd George and M. Briand, both secretly sensible, should remain colleagues at the expense of a little nonsense in unison for a short time? This view of the situation prevailed, and an ultimatum was conveyed to Germany on the following lines.[1]

The reparation payments, proposed to Germany by the Paris Conference, were made up of a determinate part and in indeterminate part. The former consisted of £100 million per annum for two years, £150 million for the next three, then £200 million for three more, and £250 million for three after that and, finally,

---

[1] The text of these Decisions is given in Appendix 2.

£300 million annually for 31 years, all these figures being in terms of gold. The latter (the indeterminate part) consisted of an annual sum, additional to the above, equal in value to 12 per cent of the German exports. The fixed payments under this scheme added up to a gross total of £11,300,000,000, which was a little less than the gross total contemplated at Boulogne but, with the export proportion added, a far greater sum.

The indeterminate element renders impossible an exact calculation of this burden, and it is no longer worth while to go into details. But I calculated at the time, without contradiction, that these proposals amounted for the normal period to a demand exceeding £400 million per annum, which is double the highest figure that any competent person here or in the United States has ever attempted to justify.

The Paris Decisions, however, coming as they did after the discussions of Boulogne and Brussels, were not meant seriously, and were simply another move in the game, to give M. Briand a breathing space. I wonder if there has ever been anything quite like it—best diagnosed perhaps as a consequence of the portentous development of 'propaganda'. The monster had escaped from the control of its authors, and the extraordinary situation was produced in which the most powerful statesmen in the world were compelled by forces, which they could not evade, to meet together day after day to discuss detailed variations of what they knew to be impossible.

Mr Lloyd George successfully took care, however, that the bark should have no immediate bite behind it. The consideration of effective penalties was postponed, and the Germans were invited to attend in London in a month's time to convey their answer by word of mouth.

M. Briand duly secured his triumph in the Chamber. 'Rarely', *The Times* reported, 'can M. Briand in all his long career as a speaker and Parliamentarian have been in better form. The flaying of M. Tardieu was intensely dramatic, even if at times almost a little painful for the spectators as well as for the victim.' M. Tardieu had overstated his case, and 'roundly asserting that the policy of France during the last year had been based on the conclusion that the financial clauses of the Treaty of Versailles could not be executed, had gained considerable applause by declaring that this was just the thesis of the pacifist, Mr Keynes, and of the German delegate, Count Brockdorff-Rantzau'—which was certainly rather unfair to the Paris Decisions. But by that date, even in France, to praise the perfections of the Treaty was to make oneself ridiculous. 'I am an ingenuous man,' said M. Briand as he mounted the tribune, 'and when I received from M. Tardieu news that he was going to interpellate me, I permitted myself to feel a little pleased. I told myself that M. Tardieu was one of the principal architects of the Treaty of Versailles, and that as such, though he knew its good qualities, he would also know its blemishes, and that he would, therefore, be indulgent to a man who had done his best in fulfilling his duty of applying it—*mais voilà* (with a gesture)—I did not stop to remember that M. Tardieu had already expended all his stock of indulgence upon his own handiwork.' The monstrous offspring of propaganda was slowly dying.

## V. THE FIRST CONFERENCE OF LONDON
### (1–7 MARCH 1921)

In Germany the Paris proposals were taken seriously and provoked a considerable outcry. But Dr Simons accepted the invitation to London and his experts got to work at a counter-proposal. 'I was in agreement', he said at Stuttgart on 13 February, 'with the representatives of Britain and France at the Brussels Conference. The Paris Conference shattered that. A catastrophe has occurred. German public opinion will never forget these figures. Now it is impossible to return to the Seydoux plan put forward at Brussels (i.e. a provisional settlement for five years), for the German people would always see enormous demands rising before them like a spectre . . . We shall rather accept unjust dictation than sign undertakings we are not firmly persuaded the German people can keep.'

On 1 March 1921 Dr Simons presented his counter-proposal to the Allies assembled in London. Like the original counter-proposal of Brockdorff-Rantzau at Versailles, it was not clear-cut or entirely intelligible; and it was rumoured that the German experts were divided in opinion amongst themselves. Instead of stating in plain language what Germany thought she could perform, Dr Simons started from the figures of the Paris Decisions and then proceeded by transparent and futile juggling to reduce them to a quite different figure. The process was as follows. Take the gross total of the fixed annuities of the Paris scheme (i.e. apart from the export proportion), namely £11,300,000,000, and calculate its present value at 8 per cent interest, namely £2,500 million; deduct from this £1,000 million as the alleged (but certainly not the actual) value of Germany's deliveries up to date, which leaves £1,500. This was the utmost Germany could pay. If the Allies could raise an international loan of £400 million, Germany would pay the interest and sinking fund on this, and in addition £50 million a year for five years, towards the discharge of the capital sum remaining over and above the £400 million, namely £1,100 million, which capital sum, however, would not carry interest pending repayment. At the end of five years the rate of repayment would be reconsidered. The whole proposal was contingent on the retention of Upper Silesia and the removal of all impediments to German trade.

The actual substance of this proposal was not unreasonable and probably as good as the Allies will ultimately secure. But the figures were far below even those of the Brussels experts, and the mode of putting it forward naturally provoked prejudice. It was summarily rejected.

Two days later Mr Lloyd George read to the German delegation a lecture on the guilt of their country, described their proposals as 'an offence and an exasperation', and alleged that their taxes were 'ridiculously low compared with Great Britain's'. He then delivered a formal declaration on behalf of the Allies that Germany was in default in respect of 'the delivery for trial of the criminals who have offended against the laws of war, disarmament, and the payment in cash or kind of £1,000 million (gold)'; and concluded with an ultimatum[1] to the effect that unless he heard by Monday (7 March) 'that Germany was either prepared to accept the Paris Decisions or to submit proposals which would be in other ways an equally satisfactory discharge of her obligations under the Treaty of Versailles (subject to the concessions made in the Paris proposals)', the Allies would proceed to (1) the occupation of Duisburg, Ruhrort, and Düsseldorf on the right bank of the Rhine, (2) a levy on all payments due to Germany on German goods sent to allied countries, (3) the establishment of a line of customs between the occupied area of Germany and the rest of Germany, and (4) the retention of the customs paid on goods entering or leaving the occupied area.

During the next few days negotiations proceeded, to no purpose, behind the scenes. At midnight on 6 March, M. Loucheur and Lord D'Abernon offered the Germans the alternative of a fixed payment of £150 million for 30 years and an export proportion of 30 per cent.[2] The formal Conference was resumed on 7 March. 'A crowd gathered outside Lancaster House in the morning and cheered Marshal Foch and Mr Lloyd George. Shouts of "Make them pay, Lloyd George!" were general. The German delegates were regarded with curiosity. General von Seeckt wore uniform with a sword. He wore also an eyeglass in the approved manner of the Prussian officer and bore himself as the incarnation of Prussian militarism. Marshal Foch, Field-Marshal Sir Henry Wilson, and the other allied soldiers also wore uniform.'[3]

Dr Simons communicated his formal reply. He would accept

[1] The full text is given in Appendix 4.
[2] Compare this with the fixed payment of £100 million and an export proportion of 26 per cent proposed in the second Ultimatum of London, only two months later.
[3] *The Times*, 8 March 1921.

the régime of the Paris Decisions as fixed for the first five years, provided Germany was helped to pay by means of a loan and retained Upper Silesia. At the end of five years the Treaty of Versailles would resume its authority, the provisions of which he preferred, as he was entitled to do, to the proposals of Paris. 'The question of war guilt is to be decided neither by the Treaty, nor by acknowledgement, nor by sanctions; only history will be able to decide the question as to who was responsible for the world war. We are all of us still too near to the event.' The sanctions threatened were, he pointed out, all of them illegal. Germany could not be technically in default in respect of reparation until the Reparation Commission had made the pronouncements due from them on 1 May. The occupation of further German territory was not lawful under the Treaty. The retention of part of the value of German goods was contrary to undertakings given by the British and Belgian governments. The erection of a special customs tariff in the Rhineland was only permissible under Article 270 of the Treaty for the protection of the economic interests of the Rhineland population and not for the punishment of the whole German people in respect of unfulfilled Treaty obligations. The arguments as to the illegality of the sanctions were indisputable, and Mr Lloyd George made no attempt to answer them. He announced that the sanctions would be put into operation immediately.

The rupture of the negotiations was received in Paris 'with a sigh of relief',[1] and orders were telegraphed by Marshal Foch for his troops to march at 7 a.m. next morning.

No new reparation scheme, therefore, emerged from the Conference of London. Mr Lloyd George's acquiescence in the Decisions of Paris had led him too far. Some measure of personal annoyance at the demeanour of the German representatives and the failure of what, in its inception, may have been intended as bluff, had ended in his agreeing to an attempt to enforce the Decisions by the invasion of Germany. The economic penalties,

---

[1] *The Times*, 8 March 1921.

whether they were legal or not, were so obviously ineffective for the purpose of collecting money, that they can hardly have been intended for that purpose, and were rather designed to frighten Germany into putting her name to what she could not, and did not intend to perform, by threatening a serious step in the direction of the policy, openly advocated in certain French quarters, of permanently detaching the Rhine provinces from the German Commonwealth. The grave feature of the Conference of London lay partly in Great Britain's lending herself to a further-ance of this policy, and partly in contempt for the due form and processes of law.

For it was impossible to defend the legality of the occupation of the three towns under the Treaty of Versailles.[1] Mr Lloyd George endeavoured to do so in the House of Commons, but at a later stage of the debate the contention was virtually abandoned by the Attorney-General.

The object of the Allies was to compel Germany to accept the Decisions of Paris. But Germany's refusal to accept these proposals was within her rights and not contrary to the Treaty, since they lay outside the Treaty and included features unauthor-ised by the Treaty which Germany was at liberty either to accept or to reject. It was necessary, therefore, for the Allies to find some other pretext. Their effort in this direction was perfunctory, and consisted, as already recorded, in a vague reference to war criminals, disarmament, and the payment of 20 milliard gold marks.

The allegation of default in paying the 20 milliard gold marks was manifestly untenable at that date (7 March 1921); for according to the Treaty, Germany had to pay this sum by 1 May 1921, 'in such instalments and in such manner as the Reparation Commission may fix', and in March 1921 the Reparation Commission had not yet demanded these cash

[1] A week or two later the German government made a formal appeal to the League of Nations against the legality of this act; but I am not aware that the League took any action on it.

payments.[1] But assuming that there had been technical default in respect of the war criminals and disarmament (and the original provisions of the Treaty had been so constantly modified that it was very difficult to say to what extent this was the case), it was our duty to state our charges precisely and, if penalties were threatened, to make these penalties dependent on a failure to meet our charges. We were not entitled to make vague charges, and then threaten penalties unless Germany agreed to something which had nothing to do with the charges. The Ultimatum of 7 March substituted for the Treaty the intermittent application of force in exaction of varying demands. For whenever Germany was involved in a technical breach of any one part of the Treaty the Allies were, apparently, to consider themselves entitled to make any changes they saw fit in any other part of the Treaty.

In any case the invasion of Germany beyond the Rhine was not a lawful act under the Treaty. This question became of even greater importance in the following month, when the French announced their intention of occupying the Ruhr. The legal issue is discussed in Excursus 2 at the conclusion of this chapter.

## VI. THE SECOND CONFERENCE OF LONDON
### (29 APRIL–5 MAY, 1921)

The next two months were stormy. The sanctions embittered the situation in Germany without producing any symptoms of surrender in the German government. Towards the end of March the latter sought the intervention of the United States and transmitted a new counter-proposal through the government of that country. In addition to being straightforward and more precise, this offer was materially better than that of Dr Simons in

---

[1] A few weeks later the Reparation Commission endeavoured to put the action of the Supreme Council in order, by demanding one milliard marks in gold (£50 million), that is to say, the greater part of the reserve of the Reichsbank against its note issue. This demand was afterwards dropped.

London at the beginning of the month. The chief provisions[1] were as follows:

1. The German liability to be fixed at £2,500 million (gold) present value.

2. As much of this as possible to be raised immediately by an international loan, issued on attractive terms, of which the proceeds would be handed over to the Allies, and the interest and sinking fund on which Germany would bind herself to meet.

3. Germany to pay interest on the balance at 4 per cent for the present.

4. The sinking fund on the balance to vary with the rate of Germany's recovery.

5. Germany, in part discharge of the above, to take upon herself the actual reconstruction of the devastated areas on any lines agreeable to the Allies, and in addition to make deliveries in kind on commercial lines.

6. Germany is prepared, 'up to her powers of performance', to assume the obligations of the Allies to America.

7. As an earnest of her good intentions, she offers £50 million (gold) in cash immediately.

If this is compared with Dr Simons's first offer, it will be seen that it is at least 50 per cent better, because there is no longer any talk of deducting from the total of £2,500 million an alleged (and in fact imaginary) sum of £1,000 million in respect of deliveries prior to 1 May 1921. If we assume an international loan of £250 million, costing 8 per cent for interest and sinking fund,[2] the German offer amounted to an immediate payment of £110 million per annum, with a possibility of an increase later in proportion to the rate of Germany's economic recovery.

The United States government, having first ascertained privately that this offer would not be acceptable to the Allies, refrained from its formal transmission.[3] On this account, and

[1] The full text is given in Appendix 5.
[2] The practicability of such a loan on a large scale is of course more than doubtful.
[3] The German government is reported also to have offered, alternatively, to accept any sum which the President of the United States might fix.

also because it was overshadowed shortly afterwards by the Second Conference of London, this very straightforward proposal has never received the attention it deserves. It was carefully and precisely drawn up, and probably represented the full maximum that Germany could have performed, if not more.

But the offer, as I have said, made very little impression; it was largely ignored in the press, and scarcely commented on anywhere. For in the two months which elapsed between the First and Second Conferences of London there were two events of great importance, which modified the situation materially.[1]

The first of these was the result of the Silesian plebiscite held in March 1921. The earlier German reparation offers had all been contingent on her retention of Upper Silesia; and this condition was one which, in advance of the plebiscite, the Allies were unable to accept. But it now appeared that Germany was in fact entitled to most of the country and, possibly, to the greater part of the industrial area. But this result also brought to a head the acute divergence between the policy of France and the policy of the other Allies towards this question.

The second event was the decision of the Reparation Commission, communicated to Germany on 27 April 1921, as to her aggregate liabilities under the Treaty. Allied finance ministers had foreshadowed 300 milliard gold marks; at the time of the Decisions of Paris, responsible opinion expected 160–200 milliards;[2] and the author of *The Economic Consequences of the Peace* had suffered widespread calumny for fixing on the figure of 137 milliards,[3] as being the nearest estimate he could make. The public, and the government also, were therefore taken by surprise when the Reparation Commission announced that they unanimously assessed the figure at 132 milliards (i.e. £6,600 million gold).[3] It now turned out that the Decisions of Paris, which had been represented as a material amelioration of the

---

[1] After the enforcement of the sanctions and the failure of the counter-proposals, the Cabinet of Herr Fehrenbach and Dr Simons was succeeded by that of Dr Wirth.

[2] As late as 26 January 1921, M. Doumer gave a forecast of 240 milliards.

[3] Exclusive of sums due in repayment of war loans made to Belgium.

Treaty which Germany was ungrateful not to accept, were no such thing; and that Germany was at that moment suffering from an invasion of her territory for a refusal to subscribe to terms which were severer in some respects than the Treaty itself. I shall examine the decision of the Reparation Commission in detail in chapter 4. It put the question on a new basis and the Decisions of London could hardly have been possible otherwise.

The decision of the Reparation Commission and the arrival of the date, 1 May 1921, fixed in the Treaty for the promulgation of a definite reparation scheme, provided a sufficient ground for reopening the whole question. Germany had refused the Decisions of Paris; the sanctions had failed to move her; the régime of the Treaty was therefore reinstated; and under the Treaty it was for the Reparation Commission to propose a scheme.

In these circumstances the Allies met once more in London in the closing days of April 1921. The scheme there concerted was really the work of the Supreme Council, but the forms of the Treaty were preserved, and the Reparation Commission were summoned from Paris to adopt and promulgate as their own the decree of the Supreme Council.

The Conference met in circumstances of great tension. M. Briand had found it necessary to placate his Chamber by announcing that he intended to occupy the Ruhr on 1 May. The policy of violence and illegality, which began with the Conference of Paris, had always included hitherto just a sufficient ingredient of make-believe to prevent its being as dangerous as it pretended to the peace and prosperity of Europe. But a point had now been reached when something definite, whether good or bad, seemed bound to happen; and there was every reason for anxiety. Mr Lloyd George and M. Briand had walked hand-in-hand to the edge of a precipice; Mr Lloyd George had looked over the edge; and M. Briand had praised the beauties of the prospect below and the exhilarating sensations of a descent. Mr Lloyd George, having indulged to the full his habitual morbid taste for looking over, would certainly end in drawing back, explaining at the same time how much he sympathised with M. Briand's standpoint. But would M. Briand?

In this atmosphere the Conference met and, considering all the circumstances, including the past commitments of the principals, the result was on the whole a victory for good sense, not least because the Allies there decided to return to the pathway of legality within the ambit of the Treaty. The new proposals concerted at this Conference were, whether they were practicable or not in execution, a lawful development of the Treaty, and in this respect sharply distinguished from the Decisions of Paris in the January preceding. However bad the Treaty might be, the London scheme provided a way of escape from a policy worse even than that of the Treaty—acts, that is, of arbitrary lawlessness based on the mere possession of superior force.

In one respect the Second Ultimatum of London was lawless; for it included an illegal threat to occupy the Ruhr valley if Germany refused its terms. But this was for the sake of M. Briand, whose minimum requirement was that he should at least be able to go home in a position to use, for conversational purposes, the charms of the precipice from which he was hurrying away. And the Ultimatum made no demand on Germany to which she was not already committed by her signature to the Treaty.

For this reason the German government was right, in my judgement, to accept the Ultimatum unqualified, even though it still included demands impossible of fulfilment. For good or ill Germany had signed the Treaty. The new scheme added nothing to the Treaty's burdens and, although a reasonable permanent settlement was left where it was before—in the future—in some respects it abated them. Its ratification, in May 1921, was in conformity with the Treaty, and merely carried into effect what Germany had had reason to anticipate for two years past. It did not call on her to do immediately—that is to say, in the course of the next six months—anything incapable of performance. It wiped out the impossible liability under which she lay of paying forthwith a balance of £600 million (gold) due under the Treaty on 1 May. And, above all, it obviated the occupation of the Ruhr and preserved the peace of Europe.

There were those in Germany who held that it must be wrong that Germany should under threats profess insincerely what she could not perform. But the submissive acceptance by Germany of a lawful notice under a Treaty she had already signed committed her to no such profession, and involved no recantation of her recent communication through the President of the United States as to what would eventually prove in her sincere belief to be the limits of practicable performance.

In the existence of such sentiments, however, Germany's chief difficulty lay. It has not been understood in England or in America how deep a wound has been inflicted on Germany's self-respect by compelling her, not merely to perform acts, but to subscribe to beliefs which she did not in fact accept. It is not usual in civilised countries to use force to compel wrongdoers to confess, even when we are convinced of their guilt; it is still more barbarous to use force, after the fashion of inquisitors, to compel adherence to an article of belief because we ourselves believe it. Yet towards Germany the Allies had appeared to adopt this base and injurious practice, and had enforced on this people at the point of the bayonet the final humiliation of reciting, through the mouths of their representatives, what they believed to be untrue.

But in the Second Ultimatum of London the Allies were no longer in this fanatical mood, and no such requirement was intended. I hoped, therefore, at the time that Germany would accept the notification of the Allies and do her best to obey it, trusting that the whole world is not unreasonable and unjust, whatever the newspapers may say; that Time is a healer and an illuminator; and that we had still to wait a little before Europe and the United States could accomplish in wisdom and mercy the economic settlement of the war.

## EXCURSUS 1

### COAL

The question of coal has considerable importance for reparation, both because (in spite of the exaggerations of the Treaty) it is a form in which Germany can make important payments, and also because of the reaction of coal deliveries on Germany's internal economy. Up to the middle of 1921 Germany's payments for reparation were almost entirely in the form of coal. And coal was the main topic of the Spa Conference, where for the first time the governments of the Allies and of Germany met face to face.

Under the terms of the Treaty Germany was to deliver 3,400,000 tons of coal per month. For reasons explained in detail in *The Economic Consequences of the Peace* [*JMK*, vol. II, 51–61] this total was a figure of rhetoric and not capable of realisation. Accordingly for the first quarter of 1920 the Reparation Commission reduced their demand to 1,660,000 tons per month, and in the second quarter to 1,500,000 tons per month; whilst in the second quarter Germany actually delivered at the rate of 770,000 tons per month. This last figure was unduly low, and by the latter date coal was in short supply throughout the world and very dear. The main object of the Spa Coal Agreement was, therefore, to secure for France an increased supply of German coal.

The Conference was successful in obtaining coal, but on terms not unfavourable to Germany. After much bargaining the deliveries were fixed at 2 million tons a month for six months from August 1920. But the German representatives succeeded in persuading the Allies that they could not deliver this amount unless their miners were better fed and that this meant foreign credit. The Allies agreed, therefore, to *pay* Germany something substantial for this coal, the sums thus received to be utilised in purchasing from abroad additional food for the miners. In form, the greater part of the sum thus paid was a loan; but, since it was set off as a prior charge against the value of reparation deliveries (e.g. the ships), it really amounted to paying back to Germany the value of a part of these deliveries. Germany's total cash receipts[1] under these arrangements actually came to about 360 million gold marks,[2] which worked out at about 40s per ton averaged over the whole of the deliveries. As at this time the German internal price was from 25s to 30s per ton, the German government received in foreign currency substantially more than they had to pay for the coal to the home producers. The high figure of 2 million tons per month involved short supplies to German transport and industry. But the money was badly wanted, and was of the utmost assistance in paying for the German food programme (and also in meeting German liabilities in respect of pre-war debts) during the autumn and winter of 1920.

This is a convenient point at which to record the subsequent history of the coal deliveries. During the next six months Germany very nearly fulfilled the Spa Agreement, her deliveries towards the 2 million tons per month being 2,055,227 tons in August, 2,008,470 tons in September, 2,288,049 tons in October, 1,912,696 tons in November, 1,791,828 tons in December, and 1,678,675 tons in January 1921. At the end of January 1921 the Spa Agreement lapsed, and since that time Germany has had to continue her coal deliveries without any payment or advance of cash in return for them. To make up for the accumulated deficit under the Spa Agreement, the Reparation Commission called for 2,200,000 tons per month in February and March, and continued to demand this figure in subsequent months. Like so much else, however, this demand was only on paper. Germany was not able to fulfil it, her actual deliveries during the next six months

[1] Under the Spa Agreement (see Appendix 1) Germany was to be paid in cash 5 gold marks per ton for *all* coal delivered, and, in the case of coal delivered *overland*, 'lent' (i.e. advanced out of reparation receipts) the difference between the German inland price and the British export price. At the date of the Spa Conference this difference was about 70s per ton (100s less 30s), but this sum was not to be advanced in the case of the undetermined amount of coal delivered *by sea*. The advances were made by the Allies in the proportions 61 per cent by France, 24 per cent by Great Britain, and 15 per cent by Belgium and Italy.

[2] For details of these payments see p. 85.

amounting to 1,885,051 tons in February 1921, 1,419,654 tons in March, 1,510,332 tons in April, 1,549,768 tons in May, 1,453,761 tons in June, and 1,399,132 tons in July. And the Reparation Commission, not really wanting the coal, tacitly acquiesced in these quantities. During the first half of 1921 there was, in fact, a remarkable reversal of the situation six months earlier. In spite of the British coal strike, France and Belgium, having replenished their stocks and suffering from a depression in the iron and steel trades, were in risk of being glutted with coal. If Germany had complied with the full demands of the Reparation Commission the recipients would not have known what to do with the deliveries. Even as it was, some of the coal received was sold to exporters, and the coal miners of France and Belgium were in danger of short employment.

The statistics of the aggregate German output of pit coal are now as follows, exclusive of Alsace-Lorraine, the Saar, and the Palatinate, in million tons:

|  | 1913 | 1917 | 1918 | 1919 | 1920 | 1921 (first nine months) |
|---|---|---|---|---|---|---|
| Germany exclusive of Upper Silesia | 130·19 | 111·66 | 109·54 | 92·76 | 99·66 | 76·06 |
| Germany inclusive of Upper Silesia | 173·62 | 154·41 | 148·19 | 117·69 | 131·35 | 100·60 |
| Per cent of 1913 output | 100 | 88·9 | 85·4 | 67·8 | 75·7 | 77·2 |

The production of rough lignite (I will not risk controversy by attempting to convert this into its pit-coal equivalent) rose from 87·1 million tons in 1913 to 93·8 in 1919, 111·6 in 1920, and 90·8 in the first three quarters of 1921.

The Spa Agreement supplied a temporary palliative of the anomalous conditions governing the *price* at which these coal deliveries are credited to Germany. But with the termination of this Agreement they again require attention. Under the Treaty Germany is credited in the case of coal delivered *overland* with 'the German pithead price to German nationals' plus the freight to the frontier; and in the case of coal delivered *by sea* with the export price; provided in each case this price is not in excess of the British export price. Now for various internal reasons the German government have thought fit to maintain the pithead price to German nationals far below the world price, with the result that she gets credited with much less than its real value for her deliveries of reparation coal. During the year ending June 1921 the average legal maximum price of the different kinds of coal was about 270 marks a ton, inclusive of a tax of 20 per cent on the price,[1] which at the exchange then prevailing was about 20s, i.e. between a third and a half of the British price at that date. The fall in the mark exchange in the autumn of 1921 increased the discrepancy. For although the price of German coal was substantially increased in terms of paper marks, and although the price of British coal had fallen sharply, the movements of exchange so outdistanced the other factors that in November 1921 the price of British coal worked out at about three and a half times the price of the best bituminous coal from the Ruhr. Thus not only were the German ironmasters placed in an advantageous position for competing with British producers, but the Belgian and French industries also benefited artificially through the receipt by their governments of very low-priced coal.

The German government is in rather a dilemma in this matter. An increase in the coal tax is one of the most obvious sources for an increased revenue, and such a tax would be, from the standpoint of the exchequer, twice blessed, since it would increase correspondingly the reparation credits. But on the other hand, such a proposal unites two groups against them, the industrialists, who want cheap coal for industry, and the Socialists, who want cheap coal for the domestic stove. From the revenue standpoint the tax would probably stand an increase from 20 per cent to 60 per cent; but from the political standpoint an increase from 20 per cent to 30 per cent is the highest con-

---

[1] This very valuable tax, first imposed in 1917, yielded in 1920–1 4½ milliard marks.

templated at present, with a differential price in favour of domestic consumers.[1]

I take this opportunity of making a few corrections or amplifications of the passages in *The Economic Consequences of the Peace* which deal with coal.

1. The fate of Upper Silesia is highly relevant to some of the conclusions about coal in chapter 4 of *The Economic Consequences of the Peace* [*JMK*, vol. II, 52–7]. I there stated that 'German authorities claim, not without contradiction, that to judge from the votes cast at elections, one-third of the population would elect in the Polish interest, and two-thirds in the German', which forecast turned out to be in almost exact accordance with the facts. I also urged that, unless the plebiscite went in a way which I did not expect, the industrial districts ought to be assigned to Germany. But I felt no confidence, having regard to the policy of France, that this would be done; and I allowed, therefore, in my figures for the possibility that Germany would lose this area.

The actual decision of the allies, acting on the advice of the Council of the League of Nations to whom the matter had been referred, which we have discussed briefly above (pp. 6–8), divides the industrial triangle between the two claimants to it. According to an estimate of the Prussian Ministry of Trade 86 per cent of the total coal deposits of Upper Silesia fall to Poland, leaving 14 per cent to Germany. Germany retains a somewhat larger proportion of pits in actual operation, 64 per cent of the current production of coal falling to Poland and 36 per cent to Germany.[2]

The figure of 100 million tons, given in *The Economic Con-*

---

[1] Dr Wirth's first government prepared a Bill to raise the tax to 30 per cent, with power, however, to reduce the rate temporarily to 25 per cent. It was estimated that the 30 per cent tax would bring in a revenue of 9·2 milliard marks.

[2] The same authority estimates that 85·6 per cent of Upper Silesia's zinc ore production and all the zinc smelting works fall to Poland. This is of some importance, since before the war Upper Silesia was responsible for 17 per cent of the total world production of zinc. Of the iron and steel production of the area 63 per cent falls to Poland. I am not in a position to check any of these figures. Some authorities ascribe a higher proportion of the coal to Poland.

*sequences of the Peace* for the *net* German production (i.e. deducting consumption at the mines themselves) in the near future *excluding* Upper Silesia, should, therefore, be replaced by the figure of (say) 115 million tons, *including* such part of Upper Silesia as Germany is now to retain.

2. I beg leave to correct a misleading passage in a footnote [*JMK*, vol. II, 53–4, n. 3] of *The Economic Consequences of the Peace*. I there spoke of 'Poland's pre-war annual demand' for coal, where I should have said 'pre-war Poland's pre-war annual demand'. The mistake was not material, as I allowed for Germany's diminished requirements for coal, due to loss of territory, in the body of the text. But I confess that the footnote, as published, might be deemed misleading. At the same time it is, I think, a tribute to the general accuracy of *The Economic Consequences* that partisan critics should have fastened so greedily on the omission of the word 'pre-war' before the word 'Poland' in the footnote in question. Quite a considerable literature has grown up round it. The Polish Diet devoted 20 January 1921 to the discussion and patriotic analysis of this footnote, and concluded with a Resolution ordering the chief speech of the occasion (that of Deputy A. Wiersbicki) to be published throughout the world in several languages at the expense of the state. I apologise for any depreciation in the Polish mark for which I may have been so inadvertently responsible. Mr Wiersbicki begins: 'A book appeared by Keynes . . . the author of a well-known work on India, that pearl of the English crown, that land which is a beloved subject of study to the English. Through such studies a man may win himself name and fame'—which was certainly a little unscrupulous of me. And he concludes:

But England too must believe in facts! And if Keynes, whose book is impregnated with a humanitarian spirit and with understanding of the necessity to get up beyond selfish interests, if Keynes is convinced by actual data that he has done a wrong, that he has wrought confusion in the ideas of statesmen and politicians as regards Upper Silesia, then he too will see with his eyes and must become the friend of Poland, of Poland as an active factor in the development of the natural wealth of Silesia.

I owe it to so generous and eloquent a critic to quote the corrected figures, which are as follows: the Polish lands, united by the Peace Treaty into the new Polish state, consumed in 1913 19,445,000 tons of coal, of which 8,989,000 tons were produced within that area and 7,370,000 tons were imported from Upper Silesia (the total production of Upper Silesia in that year being 43,800,000 tons).[1] The Silesian Plebiscite has been preceded and followed by a mass of propagandist literature on both sides. For the economic questions involved see, particularly, on the Polish side: Wiersbicki, *The Truth about Upper Silesia*; Olszewski, *Upper Silesia, Her Influence on the Solvability and on the Economic Life of Germany*, and *The Economic Value of Upper Silesia for Poland and Germany respectively*; and on the German side: Sidney Osborne, *The Upper Silesian Question and Germany's Coal Problem*; *The Problem of Upper Silesia* (papers by various authors, not all on the German side, with excellent maps, edited by Sidney Osborne); various pamphlets by Professor Schulz-Gavernitz, and documents circulated by the Breslau Chamber of Commerce.

3. My observations on Germany's capacity to deliver reparation coal have been criticised in some quarters[2] on the ground that I made insufficient allowance for the compensation which is available to her by the more intensive exploitation of her deposits of lignite or brown coal. This criticism is scarcely fair, because I was the first in popular controversy to call attention to the factor of lignite, and because I was careful from the outset to disclaim expert knowledge of the subject.[3] I still find it difficult, in the face of conflicting expert opinions, to know how much importance

---

[1] These are the figures according to the Polish authorities. But it is difficult to obtain accurate pre-war figures for an area which was not coterminous with any then existing state; and these totals have been questioned in detail by Dr W. Schotte.

[2] See e.g. my controversy with M. Brenier in *The Times*.

[3] In *The Economic Consequences of Peace* (*JMK*, vol. II, 57 n. 3), I wrote as follows: 'The reader must be reminded in particular that the above calculations take no account of the German production of lignite . . . I am not competent to speak on the extent to which the loss of coal can be made good by the extended use of lignite or by economies in its present employment; but some authorities believe that Germany may obtain substantial compensation for her loss of coal by paying more attention to her deposits of lignite.'

to attach to this material. Since the Armistice there has been a substantial increase in output, which was 36 per cent higher in the first half of 1921 than in 1913.[1] In view of the acute shortage of coal this output must have been of material assistance towards meeting the situation. The deposits are near the surface, and no great amount of capital or machinery is needed for its production. But lignite briquette is a substitute for coal for certain purposes only, and the evidence is conflicting as to whether any further material expansion is economically practicable.[2]

The process of briquetting the rough lignite is probably a wasteful one, and it is doubtful whether it would be worth while to set up *new* plant with a view to production on a larger scale. Some authorities hold that the real future of lignite and its value as an element in the future wealth of Germany lie in improved methods of *distillation* (the chief obstacle to which, as also to other uses, lies in its high water content), by which the various oils, ammonia and benzine, latent in it can be released for commercial uses.

It is certainly the case that the future possibilities of lignite should not be overlooked. But there is a tendency at present, just as was the case with potash some little time ago, to exaggerate its importance greatly as a decisive factor in the wealth-producing capacity of Germany.

[1] That is to say, production in the middle of 1921 was at the rate of about 120 million tons per annum. At that time the legal maximum price was 60 paper marks per ton (i.e. 5s or less); so that the national *profit* on the output in terms of money cannot have been a very material amount.

[2] In order to secure the increased output the number of miners was increased much more than in proportion, namely from 59,000 in 1913 to 171,000 in the first half of 1921. As a result, the cost of production of lignite rose much faster than that of coal. Also since its calorific value is much less than that of coal per unit of weight (even when it is briquetted), it can only compete with coal, unless it is assisted by preferential freight rates, within a limited area in the neighbourhood of the mines.

3-2

## EXCURSUS 2

### THE LEGALITY OF OCCUPYING GERMANY
### EAST OF THE RHINE

The years 1920 and 1921 have been filled with excursions and with threats of excursions by the French army into Germany east of the Rhine. In March 1920 France, without the approval of her Allies, occupied Frankfurt and Darmstadt. In July 1920 a threat to invade Germany by the Allies as a whole was successful in enforcing the Spa Agreement. In March 1921 a similar threat was unsuccessful in securing assent to the Paris Decisions, and Duisburg, Ruhrort, and Düsseldorf were occupied accordingly. In spite of the objections of her Allies France continued this occupation when, by the acceptance of the second Ultimatum of London, the original occasion for it had disappeared, on the ground that so long as the Upper Silesian question was un-settled, it was in the opinion of Marshal Foch just as well to retain this hold.[1] In April 1921 the French government announced their intention of occupying the Ruhr, though they were prevented from carrying this out by the pressure of the other Allies. In May 1921 the Second Ultimatum of London was successfully enforced by a threat to occupy the Ruhr valley. Thus, within the space of little more than a year the invasion of Germany, beyond the Rhine, was threatened five times and actually carried out twice.

We are supposed to be at peace with Germany, and the invasion of a country in time of peace is an irregular act, even when the invaded country is not in a position to resist. We are also bound by our adhesion to the League of Nations to avoid such action. It is, however, the contention of France, and apparently, from time to time, that of the British government

---

[1] At the Paris Conference of August 1921 Lord Curzon tried unavailingly to persuade France to abandon this illegal occupation. The so-called 'economic sanctions' were raised on 1 October 1921. The occupation still continues, though both the above pretexts have now disappeared.

also, that these acts are in some way permissible under the Treaty of Versailles, whenever Germany is in technical default in regard to any part of the Treaty, that is to say, since some parts of the Treaty are incapable of literal fulfilment, at any time. In particular the French government maintained in April 1921 that so long as Germany possessed any tangible assets, she was in voluntary default in respect of reparation, and that if she was in voluntary default any Ally was entitled to invade and pillage her territory without being guilty of an act of war. In the previous month the Allies as a whole had argued that default under chapters of the Treaty, other than the reparation chapter, also justified invasion.

Though the respect shown for legality is now very small, the legal position under the Treaty deserves nevertheless an exact examination.

The Treaty of Versailles expressly provides for breaches by Germany of the *reparation* chapter. It contains no special provision for breaches of other chapters, and such breaches are, therefore, in exactly the same position as breaches of any other Treaty. Accordingly, I will discuss separately default in respect of reparation, and other defaults.

Sections 17 and 18 of the reparation chapter, Annex II, run as follows:

'(17) In case of default by Germany in the performance of any obligation under this part of the present Treaty, the Commission will forthwith give notice of such default to each of the interested Powers, and will make such recommendations as to the action to be taken in consequence of such default as it may think necessary.

'(18) The measures which the Allied and Associated Powers shall have the right to take in case of voluntary default by Germany, and which Germany agrees not to regard as acts of war, may include economic and financial prohibitions and reprisals, and in general such other measures as the respective Governments may determine to be necessary in the circumstances.'

There is also a provision in Article 430 of the Treaty, by which any part of the occupied area which has been evacuated may be reoccupied if Germany fails to observe her obligations with regard to reparation.

The French government base their contention on the words 'and in general such other measures' in §18, arguing that this gives them an entirely free hand. The sentence taken as a whole, however, supports, on the principle of *ejusdem generis*, the interpretation that the other measures contemplated are of the nature of economic and financial reprisals. This view is confirmed by the fact that the rest of the Treaty narrowly limits the rights of occupying German territory, which, as M. Tardieu's book shows, was the subject of an acute difference of opinion between France and her Associates at the Peace Conference. There is *no* provision for occupying territory on the *right* bank of the Rhine; and the only provision for occupation in the event of default is that contained in Article 430. This Article, which provides for *re-occupation* of the *left* bank in the event of default, would have been entirely pointless and otiose if the French view were correct. Indeed the theory, that at any time during the next thirty years any Ally can invade any part of Germany on the ground that Germany has not fulfilled every letter of the Treaty, is on the face of it unreasonable.

In any case, however, §§17, 18 of Annex II of the reparation chapter only operate after a specific procedure has been set on foot by the Reparation Commission. It is the duty of the Reparation Commission to give notice of the default to each of the interested Powers, including presumably the United States, and to recommend action. If the default is voluntary—there is no provision as to who is to decide this—then the paragraphs in question become operative. There is no warrant here for isolated action by a single Ally. And indeed the Reparation Commission have never so far put this procedure in operation.

If, on the other hand, Germany is alleged to be in default under some other chapter of the Treaty, then the Allies have no recourse except to the League of Nations; and they are bound to bring into operation Article 17 of the Covenant, which provides for the case of a dispute between a member of the League and a non-member. That is to say, apart from procedure by the Reparation Commission as set forth above, breaches or alleged breaches of this Treaty are in precisely the same position as breaches of any other treaty between two Powers which are at peace.

According to Article 17, in the event of a dispute between a member of the League and a state which is not a member of the League, the latter 'shall be invited to accept the obligations of membership in the League for the purposes of such dispute, upon such conditions as the Council may deem just. If such invitation is accepted, the provisions of Articles 12 to 16 inclusive shall be applied, with such modifications as may be deemed necessary by the Council. Upon such invitation being given, the Council shall immediately institute an inquiry into the circumstances of the dispute, and recommend such action as may seem best and most effectual in the circumstances.'

Articles 12 to 16 provide, amongst other things, for arbitration in any case of 'disputes as to the interpretation of a Treaty; as to any question of international law; as to the existence of any fact which, if established, would constitute a breach of any international obligation; or as to the extent and nature of the reparation to be made for any such breach'.

The Allies as signatories of the Treaty and of the Covenant are therefore absolutely precluded, in the event of a breach or alleged breach by Germany of the Treaty, from proceeding except under the power given to the Reparation Commission as stated above, or under Article 17 of the Covenant. Any other act on their part is illegal.

In any case it is *obligatory* on the Council of the League, under Article 17, to invite Germany, in the event of a dispute between Germany and the Allies, to accept the obligations of membership in the League for the purposes of such dispute, and to institute immediately an inquiry into the circumstances of the dispute.

In my opinion the protest addressed by the German government to the Council of the League of Nations in March 1921 was correctly argued. But, as with the inclusion of pensions in the Reparation Bill, we reserve the whole stock of our indignation over illegality between nations for the occasions when it is the fault of others. I am told that to object to this is to overlook 'the human element' and is therefore both wrong and foolish.

# Chapter 3

# THE BURDEN OF THE
# LONDON SETTLEMENT

The settlement of reparations communicated to Germany by the Allied Powers on 5 May 1921, and accepted a few days later, constitutes the definitive scheme under the Treaty according to which Germany for the next two generations is to discharge her liabilities.[1] It will not endure. But it is the *fait accompli* of the hour and, therefore, deserves examination.[2]

The settlement falls into three parts, comprising (1) provisions for the delivery of bonds; (2) provisions for setting up in Berlin an Allied Committee of Guarantees; (3) provisions for actual payment in cash and kind.

1. *The delivery of bonds.* These provisions are the latest variant of similar provisions in the Treaty itself. Allied finance ministers have encouraged themselves (or their constituents) with the hope that some part of the capital sum of Germany's liabilities might be anticipated by the sale to private investors of bonds secured on future reparation payments. For this purpose it was necessary that Germany should deliver negotiable bonds. These bonds do not constitute any *additional* burden on Germany. They are simply documents constituting a title to the sums which, under other clauses, Germany is to pay over annually to the Reparation Commission.

The advantages to the Allies of marketing such bonds are obvious. If they could get rid of the bonds they would have

---

[1] The preamble states that the settlement is 'in accordance with Article 233 of the Treaty of Versailles'. This article prescribes that the scheme of payments shall provide for the discharge of the liabilities within *thirty* years, any unpaid balance at the end of this period being 'postponed' or 'handled otherwise'. In the actual settlement, however, the initial limitation to thirty years has been neglected.

[2] This actual text is printed below in full, Appendix 7.

thrown the risk of Germany's default on to others; they would have interested a great number of people all over the world in Germany's not defaulting; and they would have secured the actual cash which the exigencies of their budgets demand. But the hope is illusory. When at last a real settlement is made, it may be practicable for the German government to float an international loan of moderate amount, well within the world's estimate of their minimum capacity of payment. But, though there are foolish investors in the world, it would be sanguine to believe that there are so many of such folly as to swallow at this moment on these lines a loan of vast dimensions. It costs France at the present time somewhere about 10 per cent to float a loan of modest dimensions on the New York market. As the proposed German bonds will carry 5 per cent interest and 1 per cent sinking fund, it would be necessary to reduce their price to 57 before they would yield 10 per cent including redemption. It would be very optimistic, therefore, to expect to market them at above half their par value. Even so, the world is not likely to invest in them any large proportion of its current savings, so that the whole amount even of the A bonds, specified below, could not be marketed at this price. Moreover, in so far as the service of the bonds marketed is within the *minimum* expectation of Germany's capacity to pay (as it would have to be), the financial effect on the Ally which markets the bonds is nearly the same as though they were to borrow themselves at the rate in question. Except, therefore, in the case of those Allies whose credit is inferior to Germany's, the advantage compared with borrowing on their own credit would not be very material.[1]

The details relating to the bonds are not likely, therefore, to be operative, and need not be taken very seriously. They are really a relic of the pretences of the Peace Conference days. Briefly, the arrangements are as follows:

[1] It is not competent for a single Ally (e.g. Portugal) to claim its share of the bonds and market them at the best price obtainable. Under the Treaty of Versailles, Part VIII, Annex II, 13(*b*), questions relating to the marketing of these bonds can only be settled by *unanimous* decision of the Reparation Commission.

Germany must deliver 12 milliards of gold marks (£600 million gold) in A bonds, 38 milliards (£1,900 million gold) in B bonds, and the balance of her liabilities, provisionally estimated at 82 milliards (£4,100 million gold), in C bonds. All the bonds carry 5 per cent interest and 1 per cent cumulative sinking fund. The services of the series A, B, and C constitute respectively a first, second, and third charge on the available funds. The A bonds are issued to the Reparation Commission as from 1 May 1921, and the B bonds as from 1 November 1921, but the C bonds shall not be issued (and shall not carry interest in the meantime) except as and when the Reparation Commission is of the opinion that the payments which Germany is making under the new settlement are adequate to provide their service.

It may be noticed that the service of the A bonds will cost £36 million (gold) per annum, a sum well within Germany's capacity, and the service of the B bonds will cost £114 million (gold) per annum, making £150 million altogether, a sum in excess of my own expectations of what is practicable, but not in excess of the figure at which some independent experts, whose opinion deserves respect, have estimated Germany's probable capacity to pay. It may also be noticed that the aggregate face value of the A and B bonds (£2,500 million gold) corresponds to the figure at which the German government have agreed (in their counter-proposal transmitted to the United States) that their aggregate liability might be assessed. It is probable that, sooner or later, the C bonds at any rate will be not only postponed, but cancelled.

2. *The Committee of Guarantees.* This new body, which is to have a permanent office in Berlin, is in form and status a sub-commission of the Reparation Commission. Its members consist of representatives of the Allies represented on the Reparation Commission, with a representative of the United States, if that country consents to nominate.[1] To it are assigned the various wide and indefinite powers accorded by the Treaty of Peace to

[1] The Committee is to co-opt three representatives of neutrals when a sufficient proportion of the bonds to justify their representation has been marketed on neutral Stock Exchanges.

the Reparation Commission, for the general control and super-vision of Germany's financial system. But its exact functions, in practice and in detail, are still obscure.

According to the letter of its constitution the Committee might embark on difficult and dangerous functions. Accounts are to be opened in the name of the Committee, to which will be paid over in *gold or foreign currency* the proceeds of the German customs, 26 per cent of the value of all exports, and the proceeds of any other taxes which may be assigned as a 'guarantee' for the payment of reparation. These receipts, however, chiefly accrue not in gold or foreign currency, but in paper marks. If the Committee attempts to regulate the conversion of these paper marks into foreign currencies, it will in effect become responsible for the foreign exchange policy of Germany, which it would be much more prudent to leave alone. If not, it is difficult to see what the 'guarantees' really add to the other provisions by which Germany binds herself to make payments in foreign money.

I suspect that the only real and useful purpose of the Committee of Guarantees is as an office of the Reparation Commission *in Berlin*, a highly necessary adjunct; and the clause about 'guarantees' is merely one more of the pretences which, in all these agreements, the requirements of politics intermingle with the provisions of finance. It is usual, particularly in France, to talk much about 'guarantees', by which is meant, apparently, some device for making sure that the impossible will occur. A 'guarantee' is not the same thing as a 'sanction'. When M. Briand is accused of weakness at the Second Conference of London and of abandoning France's 'real guarantees', these provisions enable him to repudiate the charge indignantly. He can point out that the Second Conference of London not only set up a Committee of Guarantees, but secured, as a new and additional guarantee, the German customs. There is no answer to that![1]

[1] And it really is an adequate rejoinder to deputies like M. Forgeot. If a partisan or a child wants a silly, harmful thing, it may be better to meet him with a silly, harmless thing than with explanations he cannot understand. This is the traditional wisdom of statesmen and nursemaids.

3. *The provisions for payment in cash and kind.* The bonds and the guarantees are apparatus and incantation. We come now to the solid part of the settlement, the provisions for payment.

Germany is to pay in each year, until her aggregate liability is discharged:

(1) Two milliard gold marks.[1]

(2) A sum equivalent to 26 per cent of the value of her exports, or alternatively an equivalent amount as fixed in accordance with any other index proposed by Germany and accepted by the Commission.

(1) is to be paid quarterly on 15 January, 15 April, 15 July, and 15 October of each year, and (2) is to be paid quarterly on 15 February, 15 May, 15 August, and 15 November of each year.

This sum, calculated on any reasonable estimate of the future value of German exports, is materially less than the original demands of the Treaty. Germany's total liability under the Treaty amounts to 138 milliard gold marks (inclusive of the liability for Belgian debt). At 5 per cent interest and 1 per cent sinking fund, the annual charge on this would be 8·28 milliard gold marks. Under the new scheme the annual value of Germany's exports would have to rise to the improbable figure of 24 milliard gold marks before she would be liable for so much as this. As we shall see below, the probable burden of the new settlement in the near future is probably not much more than half that of the Treaty.

There is another important respect in which the demands of the Treaty are much abated. The Treaty included a crushing provision by which the part of Germany's nominal liability on which she was not able to pay interest in the early years was to

---

[1] Germany's liabilities are all fixed in terms of gold marks. The value of gold in terms of sterling varies, broadly speaking, with the fluctuations in the dollar sterling exchange. The following table is convenient for converting gold marks into sterling:

| Dollar sterling exchange | Value in sterling of 2,000 gold marks |
| --- | --- |
| 4·52 | £110 |
| 4·14 | £120 |
| 3·82 | £130 |
| 3·55 | £140 |

accumulate at compound interest.[1] There is no such provision in the new scheme; the C bonds are not to carry interest until the receipts from Germany are adequate to meet their service; and the only provision relating to back interest is for the payment of *simple* interest in the event of there being a surplus out of the receipts.

In order to understand how great an advance this settlement represented it is necessary to carry our minds back to the ideas which were prevalent not very long ago. The following table is interesting, in which, in order to reduce capital sums and annual payments to a common basis of comparison, estimates in terms of capital sums are replaced by annuities of 6 per cent of their amount:

| Estimates of | In terms of annuities expressed in milliards of gold marks |
|---|---|
| 1. Lord Cunliffe and the figure given out in the British General Election of 1918[2] | 28·8 |
| 2. M. Klotz's forecast in the French Chamber, 5 September 1919 | 18 |
| 3. The assessment of the Reparation Commission, April 1921 | 8·28 |
| 4. The London Settlement, May 1921 | 4·6[3] |

The estimate of *The Economic Consequences of the Peace* (1919), namely 2 milliards, was nearly contemporaneous with M. Klotz's figure of 18 milliards. M. Tardieu recalls that, when the Peace Conference was considering whether a definite figure could be inserted in the Treaty, the lowest figure which the British and French Prime Ministers would accept, as a compromise to meet the pressure put upon them by the American representatives, corresponded to an annuity of 10·8 milliards,[4] which is nearly two and a half times the figure which they accepted two years later under the pressure, not of Americans, but of facts.

There was yet another feature in the London Settlement

[1] The effect of this provision is discussed in *The Economic Consequences of the Peace* [*JMK*,
[2] vol. II, 104–5].
 Cf. Baruch, *The Making of the Reparation and Economic Sections of the Treaty*, p. 46; and Lamont, *What Really Happened at Paris*, p. 275.
[3] Assuming exports of 10 milliards, which is double the actual figure of 1920.
[4] *The Truth about the Treaty*, p. 305.

which recommended it to moderate opinion. The dates of payment were so arranged as to reduce the burden on Germany during the first year. The Reparation year runs from 1 May in each year to 30 April in the next; but in the period 1 May 1921 to 30 April 1922 only two, instead of four, of the quarterly payments in respect of the export proportion will fall due.

No wonder, therefore, that this settlement, so reasonable in itself compared with what had preceded it, was generally approved and widely accepted as a real and permanent solution. But in spite of its importance for the time being, as a preservative of peace, as affording a breathing space, and as a transition from foolish expectations, it cannot be a permanent solution. It is, like all its predecessors, a temporising measure, which is bound to need amendment.

To calculate the total burden, it is necessary to estimate the value of German exports. In 1920 they amounted to about 5 milliard gold marks. In 1921 the volume will be greater, but this will be offset by the fact that gold prices have fallen to less than two-thirds of what they were, so that 4 to 5 milliard gold marks is quite high enough as a preliminary forecast for the year commencing 1 May 1921.[1] It is, of course, impossible to make a close estimate for later years. The figures will depend, not only on the recovery of Germany, but on the state of international trade generally, and more especially on the level of gold prices.[2] For the next two or three years, if we are to make an estimate at all, 6 to 10 milliards is, in my judgement, the best one can make.

[1] Exports for the six months May–October 1921 were valued at about 40 milliard paper marks (exclusive, I think, of deliveries of coal and payments in kind to the Allies), as against imports valued at 53 milliard paper marks. If the monthly export figures are converted into gold marks at the average exchange of the month, the exports for the six months work out at about 1,865 million gold marks, or at the rate of rather less than 4 milliard gold marks per annum.

[2] In *The Economic Consequences of the Peace* [*JMK*, vol. II, 128], I expressly premised that my estimates were based on a value of money not widely different from that existing at the date at which I wrote. Since then prices have risen and fallen back again. The same proviso is necessary in the case of the present estimates. It would have been more practical if, in fixing Germany's liability in terms of money for a long period of years, some provision had been made for adjusting the real burden in accordance with fluctuations in the value of money during the period of payment.

Twenty-six per cent of exports, valued at 6 milliards gold, will amount to about 1½ milliard gold marks, making, with the fixed annual payment of 2 milliards, 3½ milliards altogether. If exports rise to 10 milliards, the corresponding figure is 4½ milliards. The table of payments in the near future is then as shown below, all the figures being in terms of milliards of gold marks. In the case of payments after 1 May 1922 I give alternative estimates on the basis of exports on the scale of 6 and 10 milliards respectively.

|  | 1921–2 (exports 4 milliards) | 1922–3 and subsequently (exports 6 milliards) | 1922–3 and subsequently (exports 10 milliards) |
|---|---|---|---|
| May 25 ⎫ |  | 0·39 | 0·65 |
| July 15 ⎪ | 1·00 | 0·50 | 0·50 |
| Aug. 15 ⎬ |  | 0·39 | 0·65 |
| Oct. 15 ⎭ |  | 0·50 | 0·50 |
| Nov. 15 | 0·26 | 0·39 | 0·65 |
| Jan. 15 | 0·50 | 0·50 | 0·50 |
| Feb. 15 | 0·26 | 0·39 | 0·65 |
| April 15 | 0·50 | 0·50 | 0·50 |
| Total | 2·52 | 3·56 | 4·60 |
| Equivalent in sterling at a dollar exchange[1] of $4 = £1 | £156 million | £221 million | £286 million |

Not the whole of these sums need be paid in cash, and the value of deliveries in kind is to be credited to Germany against them. This item has been estimated as high as 1·2 to 1·4 milliard gold marks per annum. The result will chiefly depend (1) on the amount and price of the coal deliveries, and (2) on the degree of success which attends the negotiations between France and Germany for the supply by the latter of materials required for the repair of the devastated area. The value of the coal deliveries depends on factors already discussed on p. 31 above, the *price of* the coal being chiefly governed by the internal German price. At a price of 20 gold marks per ton and deliveries of 2 million tons a month (neither of which figures are likely to be exceeded, or

[1] I take this as a round figure, not as a prediction of the dollar exchange. The necessary adjustment can be made, in accordance with the actual course of exchange, by reference to the table on p. 45 above.

even reached, in the near future), coal will yield credits of 0·48 milliard gold marks. In the Loucheur–Rathenau Agreement[1] the value of deliveries in kind to France, including coal, over the next five years has been estimated at a possible total of 1·4 milliard gold marks per annum. If France receives 0·4 milliard gold marks in coal, not more than 35 per cent of the balance will be credited in the reparation account. If this were realised, the aggregate deliveries in kind might approach 1 milliard. But, for various reasons, political and economic, this figure is unlikely to be reached, and if as much as 0·75 milliard per annum is realised from coal and reconstruction deliveries, this ought to be considered a highly satisfactory result.

Now the payments were so arranged as to present no insuperable difficulties during 1921. The instalment of 31 August 1921 (which did not exceed the sum which the Germans had themselves offered for immediate payment in their counter-proposal of April 1921) was duly paid, partly out of foreign balances accumulated before 1 May last, partly by selling out paper marks over the foreign exchanges, and partly by temporary advances from an international group of bankers. The instalment of 15 November 1921 was covered by the value of deliveries of coal and other material subsequent to 1 May 1921. Even the instalments of 15 January and 15 February 1922 might be covered out of further deliveries, temporary advances, and the foreign assets of German industrialists, if the German government could get hold of them. But the payment of 15 April 1922 must present more difficulty; whilst further instalments follow quickly on 15 May, 15 July, and 15 August. Some time between February and August 1922 Germany will succumb to an inevitable default. This is the maximum extent of our breathing space.[2]

---

[1] See Excursus 3.

[2] I first published this prediction in August 1921. As this book goes to press, the German government have notified the Reparation Commission (15 December 1921) that, having failed in their attempt to secure a foreign loan, they cannot find, apart from deliveries in kind, more than 150 or 200 million gold marks towards the instalments of January and February 1922. On 13 January 1922, after the Cannes Conference, the Reparation Commission gave Germany the moratorium which I reproduce in Appendix 10.

That is to say, in so far as she depends for payment (as in the long run she must do) on current income. If capital, non-recurrent resources become available, the above conclusion will require modification accordingly. Germany still has an important capital asset untouched—the property of her nationals now sequestered in the hands of the Enemy-Property Custodian in the United States, of which the value is rather more than 1 milliard gold marks. If this were to become available for reparation, directly or indirectly, default could be delayed correspondingly.[1] Similarly the grant to Germany of foreign credits on a substantial scale, even three months' credits from bankers on the security of the Reichsbank's gold, would postpone the date a little, however useless in the long run.

In reaching this conclusion, one can approach the problem from three points of view: (1) the problem of paying outside Germany, that is to say, the problem of exports and the balance of trade; (2) the problem of providing for payment by taxation, that is to say, the problem of the budget; (3) the proportion of the sums demanded to the German national income. I will take them in turn, confining myself to what Germany can be expected to perform in the near future, to the exclusion of what she might do in hypothetical circumstances many years hence.

(1) In order that Germany may be able to make payments abroad, it is necessary, not only that she should have exports, but that she should have a surplus of exports over imports. In 1920, the last complete year for which figures are available, so

[1] The United States has the right to retain and liquidate all property, rights, and interests belonging to German nationals and lying within the territories, colonies, and possessions of the United States on 10 January 1920. The proceeds of such liquidation are at the disposal of the United States 'in accordance with its laws and regulations', that is to say, at the disposal of Congress within the limitations of the Constitution, and may be applied by them in any of the three following ways: (1) the assets in question may be returned to their original German owners; (2) they may be applied to the discharge of claims by United States nationals with regard to their property, rights, and interests in German territory, or debts owing to them by German nationals, or to the payment of claims growing out of acts of the German government after the United States entered the war, and also to the discharge of similar American claims in respect of those of Germany's allies against whom the United States was at war; (3) they may be turned over to the Reparation Commission as a credit to Germany.

far from a surplus there was a deficit, the exports being valued at about 5 milliard gold marks and the imports at 5·4 milliards. The figures for 1921 so far available indicate, not an improvement, but a deterioration. The myth that Germany is carrying on a vast and increasing export trade is so widespread, that the actual figures for the six months from May to October 1921, converted into gold marks, may be given with advantage:

| | Million paper marks | | Million gold marks[1] | | |
| | Imports | Exports | Imports | Exports | Excess of imports |
|---|---|---|---|---|---|
| 1921 | | | | | |
| May | 5,487 | 4,512 | 374·4 | 307·9 | 66·5 |
| June | 6,409 | 5,433 | 388·8 | 329·7 | 59·1 |
| July | 7,580 | 6,208 | 413·7 | 338·7 | 75·0 |
| August | 9,418 | 6,684 | 477·2 | 334·8 | 142·4 |
| September | 10,668 | 7,519 | 436·6 | 307·7 | 128·9 |
| October[2] | 13,900 | 9,700 | 352·6 | 246·0 | 106·6 |
| Total for six months | 53,462 | 40,056 | 2,443·3 | 1,864·8 | 578·5 |

In respect of these six months Germany must make a fixed payment of 1,000 million gold marks plus 26 per cent of the exports as above, namely 484·8 million gold marks, that is 1,484·8 million gold marks altogether, which is equal to about 80 per cent of her exports; whereas apart from any reparation payments, she had a *deficit* on her foreign trade at the rate of more than 1 milliard gold marks per annum. The bulk of Germany's imports are necessary either to her industries or to the food supply of the country. It is therefore certain that with exports of (say) 6 milliards she could not cut her imports so low as to have the surplus of 3½ milliards, which would be necessary to meet her reparation liabilities. If, however, her exports were to rise to 10 milliards, her reparation liabilities would become 4·6 milliards. Germany, to meet her liabilities, must therefore raise the gold-value of her exports to double what they were in 1920 and 1921 *without increasing her imports at all.*

[1] The rates for conversion of paper marks into gold marks have been taken as follows: number of paper marks per 100 gold marks in May 1,465·5, June 1,647·9, July 1,832, August 1,996·4, September 2,443·2, October 3,942·6. [2] Provisional figures.

I do not say that this is impossible, given time and an over-whelming motive, and with active assistance by the Allies to Germany's export industries; but does anyone think it practicable or likely in the actual circumstances of the case? And if Germany succeeded, would not this vast expansion of exports, unbalanced by imports, be considered by our manufacturers to be her crowning crime? That this should be the case even under the London Settlement of 1921 is a measure of the ludicrous folly of the figures given out in the General Election of 1918, which were six times as high again.

(2) Next there is the problem of the budget. For reparation payments are a liability of the German *government* and must be covered by taxation. At this point it is necessary to introduce an assumption as to the relation between the gold mark and the paper mark. For whilst the liability is fixed in terms of gold marks, the revenue (or the bulk of it) is collected in terms of paper marks. The relation is a very fluctuating one, best measured by the exchange value of the paper mark in terms of American gold dollars. This fluctuation is of more importance over short periods than in the long run. For in the long run *all* values in Germany, including the yield of taxation, will tend to adjust themselves to an appreciation or depreciation in the value of the paper mark outside Germany. But the process may be a very slow one and, over the period covered by a year's budget, unanticipated fluctuations in the ratio of the gold to the paper mark may upset entirely the financial arrangements of the German Treasury.

This disturbance has of course occurred on an unprecedented scale during the latter half of 1921. Taxation in terms of paper marks, which was heavy when the £ sterling was worth 200 paper marks, becomes very inadequate when the £ sterling is worth 1,000 paper marks; but it is beyond the power of any finance minister to adjust taxation to such a situation quickly. In the first place, when the fall in the external value of the mark is proceeding rapidly, the corresponding fall in the internal value lags far behind. Until this adjustment has taken place, which may occupy a considerable time before it is complete, the taxable capacity of the people, measured in gold, is less than it was before. But even then a further interval must elapse before the gold-value of the *yield* of taxation collectable in paper marks can catch up. The experience of the British Inland Revenue Department well shows that the yield of direct taxation must largely depend on the taxable assessments of the *previous* period.

For these reasons the collapse of the mark exchange must, if it persists, destroy beyond repair the budget of 1921–2, and probably that of the first half of 1922–3 also. But I should be overstating my argument if I were to base my conclusions on the figures current at the end of 1921. In the shifting sands in which the mark is foundering it is difficult to find for one's argument any secure foothold.

During the summer of 1921 the gold mark was worth, in round figures, 20 paper marks. The internal purchasing power of the paper mark for the purposes of working-class consumption was still nearly double its corresponding value abroad, so that one could scarcely say that equilibrium had been established. Nevertheless, the position was very well adjusted compared with what it has since become. As I write (December 1921) the gold mark has been fluctuating between 45 and 60 paper marks, while the purchasing power of the paper mark inside Germany is for general purposes perhaps three times what it is outside Germany.

Since my figures of government revenue and expenditure are based on statements made in the summer of 1921, perhaps my best course is to take a figure of 20 paper marks to the gold mark. The effect of this will be to understate my argument rather than the contrary. The reader must remember that, if the mark remains at its present exchange value long enough for internal values to adjust themselves to that rate, the items in the following account, the income and the outgoings and the deficit, will all tend to be multiplied threefold.

At this ratio (of 20 paper marks = 1 gold mark) a reparation

53

liability of $3\frac{1}{2}$ milliard gold marks (assuming exports on the scale of 6 milliards) is equivalent to 70 milliard paper marks, and a liability of $4\frac{1}{2}$ milliards (assuming exports of 10 milliards) is equivalent to 90 milliard paper marks. The German budget for the financial year 1 April 1921 to 31 March 1922 provided for an expenditure of 93·5 milliards, exclusive of reparation payments, and for a revenue of 59 milliards.[1] Thus the present reparation demand would by itself absorb more than the whole of the existing revenue. Doubtless expenditure can be cut down, and revenue somewhat increased. But the budget will not cover even the lower scale of the reparation payments unless expenditure is halved and revenue doubled.[2]

If the German budget for 1922–3 manages to balance, *apart* from any provision for reparation, this will represent a great effort and a considerable achievement. Apart, however, from the technical financial difficulties, there is a political and social aspect of the question which deserves attention here. The Allies deal with the established German government, make bargains with them, and look to them for fulfilment. The Allies do not extract payment out of individual Germans direct; they put

[1] The ordinary revenue and expenditure were estimated to balance at 48·48 milliard paper marks. The extraordinary expenditure was estimated at 59·68 milliards, making a total expenditure of 108·16 milliards. Included in this, however, were 14·6 milliards for various reparation items. These are in respect of various pre-1 May 1921 items and do not allow for payments under the London Settlement; but to avoid confusion I have deducted these from the estimate of expenditure as stated above. The extraordinary revenue was estimated at 10·5 milliards, making a total revenue of 58·98 milliards.

[2] I have allowed nothing so far for the costs of the armies of occupation which, under the letter of the Treaty, Germany is under obligation to pay in addition to the sums due for reparation proper. As these charges rank in priority ahead of reparation, and as the London Agreement does not deal with them, I think Germany is liable to be called on to pay these as they accrue in addition to the annuities fixed in the London Settlement. But I am doubtful whether the Allies intend in fact to demand this. Hitherto the expense of the armies has been so great as to absorb virtually the whole of the receipts (see Excursus 5 below), having amounted by the middle of 1921 to about £200 million. In any case, it is now time that the agreement, signed at Paris in 1919 by Clemenceau, Lloyd George, and Wilson, should be brought into force, to the effect that the sum payable annually by Germany to cover the cost of occupation shall be limited to 240 million gold marks as soon as the Allies 'are convinced that the conditions of disarmament by Germany are being satisfactorily fulfilled'. If we assume that this reduced figure is brought into force, as it ought to be, the total burden on Germany for reparation and occupation comes, on the assumption of the lower figure for exports, to 3·8 milliard gold marks, that is, to 76 milliard paper marks.

pressure on the transitory abstraction called government, and leave it to this to determine and to enforce which individuals are to pay, and how much. Since at the present time the German budget is far from balancing even if there were no reparation payments at all, it is fair to say that not even a beginning has yet been made towards settling the problem of how the burden is to be distributed between different classes and different interests.

Yet this problem is fundamental. Payment takes on a different aspect when, instead of being expressed in terms of milliards and as a liability of the transitory abstraction, it is translated into a demand for a definite sum from a specific individual. This stage is not yet reached, and until it is reached the full intrinsic difficulty will not be felt. For at this stage the struggle ceases to be primarily one between the Allies and the German government and becomes a struggle between different sections and classes of Germans. The struggle will be bitter and violent, for it will present itself to each of the contesting interests as an affair of life and death. The most powerful influences and motives of self-interest and self-preservation will be engaged. Conflicting conceptions of the end and nature of society will be ranged in conflict. A government which makes a serious attempt to cover its liabilities will inevitably fall from power.

(3) What relation do the demands bear to the third test of capacity, the present income of the German people? A burden of 70 milliard paper marks (if we may, provisionally, adopt that figure as the basis of our calculations) amounts, since the population is now about 60 millions, to 1,170 marks per head for every man, woman, and child.

The great changes in money values have made it difficult, in all countries, to obtain estimates of the national income in terms of money under the new conditions. The Brussels Conference of 1920, on the basis of inquiries made in 1919 and at the beginning of 1920, estimated the German income per head at 3,900 paper marks. This figure may have been too low at the time and, on account of the further depreciation of the mark, is certainly too

55

low now. A writer in the *Deutsche Allgemeine Zeitung* (14 February 1921), working on the statistics of statutory deductions from wages and on income tax, arrived at a figure of 2,333 marks per head. This figure also is likely to be too low, partly because the statistics must mainly refer to earlier dates when the mark was less depreciated, and partly because all such statistics necessarily suffer from evasions. At the other extreme lies the estimate of Dr Albert Lansburgh who, by implication (*Die Bank*, March 1921), estimated the income per head at 6,570 marks.[1] Another recent estimate is that of Dr Arthur Heichen in the *Pester Lloyd* (5 June 1921), who put the figure at 4,450 marks. In a newspaper article published in various quarters in August 1921 I ventured to adopt the figure of 5,000 marks as the nearest estimate I could make. In fixing on this figure I was influenced by the above estimates, and also by statistics as to the general level of salaries and wages. Since then I have looked into the matter further and am still of the opinion that this figure was high enough for that date.

I am fortified in this conclusion by the result of inquiries which I addressed to Dr Moritz Elsas of Frankfurt-on-Main, on whose authority I quote the following figures. The best-known estimate of the German pre-war income is Helfferich's in his *Deutschlands Volkswohlstand 1888–1913*. In this volume he put the national income in 1913 at 40–1 milliard gold marks, *plus* 2½ milliards for net income from nationalised concerns (railways, post office, etc.), that it is say, an aggregate of 43 milliards or 642 marks per head. Starting from the figure of 41 milliards (since the national services no longer produce a profit) and deducting 15 per cent for loss of territory, we have a figure of 34·85 milliards. What multiplier ought we to apply to this in order to arrive at the present income in terms of paper marks? In 1920 commercial employes obtained on the average in terms of marks 4½ times

[1] 'This estimate is based on an average wage of about 800 paper marks monthly for male, and about 400 paper marks monthly for female, employes.' Converting these figures at the rate of 12 paper marks equal to 1 gold mark, he arrived at an aggregate national income between 30 and 34 milliard gold marks. It is not easy to see how these wage estimates, even assuming their correctness, can lead to so high an aggregate figure.

their pre-war income, whilst at that time workmen had secured an increase in their nominal wages of 50 per cent more than this, that is to say, their wages were 6 to 8 times the pre-war figure. According to the Statistische Reichsamt (*Wirtschaft und Statistik*, Heft 4, Jahrgang 1) commercial employes at the beginning of 1921 earned, males 6⅔ times and females 10 times as much as in 1913. On the basis of the same proportion as in 1920 we arrive at an increase of 10 times in the nominal wages of workmen. The wages index number of the *Frankfurter Zeitung* for August 1921 estimates the wages per hour at 11 times the pre-war level but, as the number of working hours has fallen from 10 to 8, these figures yield an increase of 8·8 times in the wage actually received. Since the wages of male commercial employes have increased less than this, since business profits in terms of paper marks only reach this figure of increase in exceptional cases, and since the income of the rentier, landlord, and professional classes has increased in a far lower proportion, an estimate of an eightfold increase in the nominal income of the country as a whole at that date (August 1921) is likely to be an over-estimate rather than an under-estimate. This leads to an aggregate national income, on the basis of the Helfferich pre-war figures, of 278·80 milliard paper marks, and to an income of 4,647 marks per head in August 1921.

No allowance is made here for the loss by war of men in the prime of life, for the loss of external income previously earned from foreign investment and the mercantile marine, or for the increase of officials. Against these omissions there may be set off the decrease of the army and the increased number of women employes.

The extreme instability of economic conditions makes it almost impossible to conduct a direct statistical inquiry into this problem at the present time. In such circumstances the general method of Dr Elsas seems to me to be the best available. His results show that the figure taken above is of the right general

[1] There are twice as many male commercial employes as there are female.

dimensions and is not likely to be widely erroneous. It enables us, too, to put an upper limit of reasonable possibility on our figures. No one, I think, would maintain that in August 1921 nominal incomes in Germany averaged 10 times their pre-war level; and 10 times Helfferich's pre-war estimate comes to 6,420 marks. *No* statistics of national incomes are very precise, but an assertion that in the middle of 1921 the German income per head per annum lay between 4,500 marks and 6,500 marks, and that it was probably much nearer the lower than the higher of these figures, say 5,000 marks, is about as near the truth as we shall get.

In view of the instability of the mark it is, of course, the case that such estimates do not hold good for any length of time and need constant revision. Nevertheless this fact does not upset the following calculation as much as might be supposed, because it operates to a certain extent on both sides of the account. If the mark depreciates further, the average income per head in paper marks will tend to rise; but in this event the equivalent in paper marks of the reparation liability will, since it is expressed in terms of *gold* marks, rise also. A real alleviation can only result from a fall in the value of *gold* (i.e. a rise in world prices).

To the taxation in respect of the reparation charge there must be added the burden of Germany's own government, central and local. By the most extreme economies, short of repudiation of war loans and war pensions, this burden could hardly be brought below 1,000 paper marks per head (at 20 paper marks = 1 gold mark), i.e. 60 milliards altogether, a figure greatly below the present expenditure. In the aggregate, therefore, 2,170 marks out of the average income of 5,000 marks, or 43 per cent, would go in taxation. If exports rise to 10 milliards (gold) and the average income to 6,000 paper marks, the corresponding figures are 2,500 marks and 42 per cent.

There are circumstances in which a wealthy nation, impelled by overwhelming motives of self-interest, might support this burden. But the annual income of 5,000 paper marks per head is equivalent in exchange value (at an exchange of 20 paper marks to 1 gold mark) to £12½ (gold), and after deduction of taxation to about £7 (gold), that is to say to less than 6d a day, which in August 1921 was the equivalent in purchasing power in Germany of something between 9d and 1s in England.[1] If Germany was given a respite, her income and with it her capacity would increase; but under her present burdens, which render saving impossible, a degradation of standards is more likely. Would the whips and scorpions of any government recorded in history have been efficient to extract nearly half their income from a people so situated?

For these reasons I conclude that whilst the Settlement of London granted a breathing space to the end of 1921, it can be no more permanent than its predecessors.

## EXCURSUS 3

### THE WIESBADEN AGREEMENT

In the summer of 1921 much interest was excited by reports of confidential interviews between M. Loucheur and Herr Rathenau, the Ministers of Reconstruction in France and Germany respectively. An agreement was provisionally reached in August 1921 and was finally signed at Wiesbaden on 6 October 1921;[2] but it does not come into force until it has received the approval of the Reparation Commission. This Commission, whilst approving the general principles underlying it, have referred it to the principal Allied governments, on the ground that it involves departures from the Treaty of Versailles beyond their own competence to authorise. The British delegate, Sir John Bradbury, has advised his government that the Agreement should be approved subject to certain modifications which he sets forth; and his report has been published.[3]

[1] For a full examination of the purchasing power of the paper mark inside Germany, see an article by M. Elsas in the *Economic Journal*, September 1921.
[2] A summary of this Agreement and other papers relating to it are given in Appendix 8.
[3] See Appendix 8.

59

The Wiesbaden Agreement is a complicated document. But the essence of it is easily explained. It falls into two distinct parts. First, it sets up a procedure by which private French firms can acquire from private German firms materials required for reconstruction in France, without France having to make payment in cash. Secondly, it provides that, whilst Germany is not to receive payment at once for any part of these goods, only a proportion of the sum due is credited to her immediately in the books of the Reparation Commission, the balance being advanced by her to France for the time being and only brought into the reparation account at a later date.

The first set of provisions has met with unqualified approval from everyone. An arrangement which may possibly stimulate payment of reparation in the form of actual materials for the reconstruction of the devastated districts satisfies convenience, economics, and sentiment in a peculiarly direct way. But such supplies were already arranged for under the Treaty, and the chief value of the new procedure lies in its replacing the machinery of the Reparation Commission by direct negotiation between the French and German authorities.[1]

The second set of provisions is, however, of a different character, since it interferes with the existing agreements between the Allies themselves as to the order and proportions which in each is to share in the available receipts from Germany, and seeks to secure for France a larger share of the earlier payments than she would receive otherwise. A priority to France is, in my opinion, desirable; but such priority should be accorded as part of a general re-settlement of reparation, in which Great Britain should waive her claim entirely. Further, the Agreement involves an act of doubtful good faith on the part of Germany. She has

[1] Incidentally the Wiesbaden Agreement sets up a fairer procedure for fixing the prices of supplies in kind than that contemplated in the Treaty. According to the Treaty the prices are fixed at the sole discretion of the Reparation Commission. In the Wiesbaden Agreement this duty is assigned to an Arbitral Commission consisting of a German representative, a French representative, and an impartial third, who are to fix the prices, broadly speaking, on the basis of price existing in France in each quarterly period subject to this price being not more than 5 per cent below the German price.

been protesting with great vehemence (and, I believe, with perfect truth) that the Decisions of London exact from her more than she can perform. But in such circumstances it is an act of impropriety for her to enter voluntarily into an agreement which must have the effect, if it is operative, of further increasing her liabilities even beyond those against which she protests as impossible. Herr Rathenau may justify his action by the arguments that this is a first step towards replacing the Decisions of London by more sensible arrangements, and also that, if he can placate Germany's largest and most urgent creditor in the shape of France, he has not much to fear from the others. M. Loucheur, on the other hand, may know as well as I do, though speaking otherwise, that the Decisions of London cannot be carried out, and that the time for a more realistic policy is at hand; he may even regard his interviews with Herr Rathenau as a foretaste of more intimate relationships between business interests on the two sides of the Rhine. But these considerations, if we were to pursue them, would lead us to a different plane of argument.

Sir John Bradbury in his report[1] on the Agreement to the British government has proposed certain modifications which would have the effect of preserving the advantages of the first set of provisions, but of nullifying the latter so far as they could operate to the detriment of France's allies.

I consider, however, that exaggerated importance has been attached to this topic, since the actual deliveries of goods made under the Wiesbaden or similar agreements are not likely to be worth such large sums of money as are spoken of. Deliveries of coal, dyestuffs, and ships, dealt with in the Annexes to Part VIII of the Treaty, are specifically excluded from the operation of the Wiesbaden Agreement, which is expressly limited to deliveries of plant and material, and these France undertakes to apply *solely* to the reconstitution of the devastated regions. The quantities of goods, which French firms and individuals will be ready to order from Germany at the full market price, and which Germany can

[1] See Appendix 8.

61

supply, for this limited purpose (so great a part of the cost of which is necessarily due to *labour* employed on the spot and not to materials capable of being imported from Germany), are not likely to amount, during the next five years, to a sum of money which the other Allies need grudge France as a priority claim.

My other reserve relates to the supposed importance of the Wiesbaden Agreement as a precedent for similar arrangements with the other Allies, and raises the general issue of the utility of arrangements for securing that Germany should pay in kind rather than in cash, for other purposes than those of the devastated areas.

It is commonly believed that, if our demands on Germany are met by her delivering to us not cash but particular commodities selected by ourselves, we can thus avoid the competition of German products against our own in the markets of the world, which must result if we compel her to find foreign currency by selling goods abroad at whatever cut in price may be necessary to market them.[1]

Most suggestions in favour of our being paid in kind are too vague to be criticised. But they usually suffer from the confusion of supposing that there is some advantage in our being paid directly in kind even in the case of articles which Germany might be expected to export in any case. For example, the Annexes to the Treaty which deal with deliveries in kind chiefly relate to coal, dyestuffs, and ships. These certainly do not satisfy the criterion of not competing with our own products; and I see very little advantage, but on the other hand some loss and inconvenience, in the Allies receiving these goods direct, instead of Germany selling them in the best market and paying over the proceeds. In the case of coal in particular, it would be much better if Germany sold her output for cash in the best export markets, whether to France and Belgium or to the neighbouring neutrals, and then paid the cash over to France and Belgium, than that coal should be delivered to the Allies for which the latter

[1] I return to the theoretical aspects of this question in chapter 6.

may have no immediate use, or by transport routes which are uneconomical, when neutrals need the coal and what the Allies really require is the equivalent cash. In some cases the Allies have re-sold the coal which Germany has delivered to them—a procedure which, in the case of an article for which freight charges cover so large a proportion of the whole value, involves a preposterous waste.

If we try to stipulate the precise commodities in which Germany is to pay us, we shall not secure from her so large a contribution, as if we fix a reasonable sum which is within her capacity, and then leave her to find the money as best she can. If, moreover, the sum fixed is reasonable, the annual payments will not be so large, in proportion to the total volume of international trade, that we need be nervous lest the payments upset the normal equilibrium of our economic life in any greater degree than is bound to result in any case from the gradual economic recovery of so formidable a trade rival as pre-war Germany.

Whilst I make these observations in the interests of scientific accuracy, I admit that projects for insisting on payment in kind may be very useful politically as a means of escaping out of our present impasse. In practice the value of such deliveries would turn out to be immensely less than the cash we are now demanding; but it may be easier to substitute deliveries of materials in place of cash, which will in practice result in a great abatement of our demands, than to abate the latter in so many words. Moreover, protests against leaving Germany free to pay us in cash by selling goods how and where she can enlist on the side of revision all the latent protectionist sentiment which still abounds. If Germany were to make a strenuous effort to pay us by exploiting the only method open to her, namely, by selling as many goods as possible at low prices all over the world, it would not be long before many minds would represent this effort as a plot to ruin us; and persons of this way of thinking will be most easily won over, if we describe a reduction in our demands, as a prohibition to Germany against developing a nefarious competitive trade.

Such a way of expressing a desirable change of policy combines, with a basis of truth, sufficient false doctrine to enable *The Times*, for example, to recommend it in a leading article without feeling conscious of any intellectual inconsistency; and it furnishes what so many people are now looking for, namely, a pretext for behaving sensibly, without having to suffer the indignity and inconvenience of thinking and speaking so too. Heaven forbid that I should discourage them! It is only too rarely that a good cause can summon to its assistance arguments sufficiently mixed to ensure success.

# EXCURSUS 4

## THE MARK EXCHANGE

The gold value of a country's inconvertible paper money may fall, either because the government is spending more than it is raising by loans and taxes and is meeting the balance by issuing paper money, or because the country is under the obligation of paying increased sums to foreigners for the purchase of investments or in discharge of debts. Temporarily it may be affected by speculation, that is to say by *anticipation*, whether well or ill founded, that one or other of the above influences will operate shortly; but the influence of speculation is generally much exaggerated, because of the immense effect which it may exercise momentarily. Both influences can only operate through the balance of debts, due for immediate payment, between the country in question and the rest of the world: the liability to make payments to foreigners operating on this directly; and the inflation of the currency operating on it indirectly, either because the additional paper money stimulates imports and retards exports, by increasing local purchasing power at the existing level of values or because the expectation that it will so act causes anticipatory speculation. The expansion of the currency can have no effect whatever on the exchanges until it reacts on

64

imports and exports, or encourages speculation; and as the latter cancels out, sooner or later, the effect of currency expansion on the exchanges can only last by reacting on imports and exports.

These principles can be applied without difficulty to the exchange value of the mark since 1920. At first the various influences were not all operating in the same direction. Currency inflation tended to depreciate the mark; so did foreign investment by Germans (the 'flight from the mark'); but investment by foreigners in German bonds and German currency (an exact line between which and short-period speculation it is not easy to draw) operated sharply in the other direction. After the mark had fallen to such a level that more than 100 marks could be obtained for a £ sterling, numerous persons all over the world formed the opinion that there would be a reaction some day to the pre-war value, and that therefore a purchase of marks or mark bonds would be a good investment. This investment proceeded on so vast a scale that it placed foreign currency at the disposal of Germany up to an aggregate value which has been estimated at from £200 million to £250 million. These resources enabled Germany, partially at least, to replenish her food supplies and to restock her industries with raw materials, requirements involving an excess of imports over exports which could not otherwise have been paid for. In addition it even enabled individual Germans to remove a part of their wealth from Germany for investment in other countries.

Meanwhile currency inflation was proceeding. In the course of the year 1920 the note circulation of the Reichsbank approximately doubled, whilst on balance the exchange value of the mark had deteriorated only slightly as compared with the beginning of that year.

Moreover, up to the end of 1920 and even during the first quarter of 1921 Germany had made no cash payments for reparation and had even *received* cash (under the Spa Agreement) for a considerable part of her coal deliveries.

After the middle of 1921, however, the various influences, which up to that time had partly balanced one another, began to work all in one direction, that is to say, adversely to the value of the mark. Currency inflation continued, and by the end of 1921 the note circulation of the Reichsbank was further increased bringing it up to nearly three times what it had been two years earlier. Imports steadily exceeded exports in value. Some foreign investors in marks began to take fright and, so far from increasing their holdings, sought to diminish them. And now at last the German government was called on to make important cash payments on reparation account. Sales of marks from Germany, instead of being absorbed by foreign investors, had now to be made in competition with sales from these same investors. Naturally the mark collapsed. It had to fall to a value at which new buyers would come forward or at which sellers would hold off.[1]

There is no mystery here, nothing but what is easily explained. The credence attached to stories of a 'German plot' to depreciate the mark wilfully is further evidence of the overwhelming popular ignorance of the influences governing the exchanges, an ignorance already displayed, to the great pecuniary advantage of Germany, by the international craze to purchase mark notes.

In its later stages the collapse has been mainly due to the necessity of paying money abroad in discharge of reparation and in repaying foreign investors in marks, with the result that the fall in the external value of the mark has outstript any figure which could be justified merely as a consequence of the present degree of currency inflation. Germany would require a much larger note issue than at present, if German internal prices were to become adjusted to gold prices at an exchange of more than 1,000 marks to the £ sterling.[2] If, therefore, the other influences

---

[1] Anyone who can fully persuade himself of the unalterable truth of the proposition that *every day* the sales of exchange must exactly equal the purchases, will have gone a long way towards understanding the secret of the exchanges.

[2] Since there are about as many German government Treasury bills, payable at short notice, held by the public and the banks, other than the Reichsbank, as there are Reichsbank notes, the note issue can be easily expanded as soon as the internal price level needs more legal tender currency to support it, even apart from new issues by the Government to meet the

were to be removed, if, that is to say, the reparation demands were revised and foreign investors were to take heart again, a sharp recovery might occur. On the other hand, a serious attempt by Germany to meet the reparation demands would cause the expenditure of her government to exceed its income by so great an amount, that currency inflation and the internal price level would catch up in due course the external depreciation in the mark.

In either event Germany is faced with an unfortunate prospect. If the present exchange depreciation persists and the internal price level becomes adjusted to it, the resulting redistribution of wealth between different classes of the community will amount to a social catastrophe. If, on the other hand, there is a recovery in the exchange, the cessation of the existing artificial stimulus to industry and of the Stock Exchange boom based on the depreciating mark may lead to a financial catastrophe.[1] Those responsible for the financial policy of Germany have a problem of incomparable difficulty in front of them. Until the reparation liability has been settled reasonably, it is scarcely worth the while of anyone to trouble his head about a problem which is insoluble. When stabilisation has become a practicable policy, the wisest course will probably be to stabilise at whatever level prices and trade seem most nearly adjusted to at that date.

excess of their expenditure over their income. Do those, who would enforce on the German government a cessation of 'the printing press', intend that the outstanding treasury bills should be repudiated, if at their maturity the holders wish to be paid off in cash? There is no such easy solution of the overwhelming problems of German public finance.

[1] Furthermore, every improvement in the value of the mark increases the real burden of what Germany owes to foreign holders of marks and also the real burden of the public debt on the Exchequer. A rate of exchange exceeding 1,000 marks to the £ has at least this advantage, that it has reduced these two burdens to very moderate dimensions.

# Chapter 4

# THE REPARATION BILL

The Treaty of Versailles specified the classes of damage in respect of which Germany was to pay reparation. It made no attempt to assess the amount of this damage. This duty was assigned to the Reparation Commission, who were instructed to notify their assessment to the German government on or before 1 May 1921.

An attempt was made during the Peace Conference to agree to a figure there and then for insertion in the Treaty. The American delegates in particular favoured this course. But an agreement could not be reached. There was no reasonable figure which was not seriously inadequate to popular expectations in France and the British Empire.[1] The highest figure to which the Americans would agree, namely, 140 milliard gold marks, was, as we shall see below, not much above the eventual assessment of the Reparation Commission; the lowest figure to which France and Great Britain would agree, namely, 180 milliard gold marks, was, as it has turned out, much above the amount to which they were entitled even under their own categories of claim.[2]

Between the date of the Treaty and the announcement of its decision by the Reparation Commission, there was much controversy as to what this amount should be. I propose to review some of the details of this problem, because, if men are in any way actuated by veracity in international affairs, a just opinion about it is still relevant to the reparation problem.

The main contentions of *The Economic Consequences of the Peace* were these: (1) that the claims against Germany which the

---

[1] A fairly adequate account of this controversy during the Peace Conference can be pieced together from the following passages: Baruch, *Making of Reparation and Economic Sections of the Treaty*, pp. 45–55; Lamont, *What Really Happened at Paris*, pp. 262–5; Tardieu, *The Truth about the Treaty*, pp. 294–309.

[2] For these figures see Tardieu, *op. cit.* p. 305.

Allies were contemplating were impossible of payment; (2) that the economic solidarity of Europe was so close that the attempt to enforce these claims might ruin everyone; (3) that the money cost of the damage done by the enemy in France and Belgium had been exaggerated; (4) that the inclusion of pensions and allowances in our claims was a breach of faith; and (5) that our legitimate claim against Germany was within her capacity to pay.

I have made some supplementary observations about (1) and (2) in chapters 3 and 6. I deal with (3) here and in chapter 5 with (4). These latter are still important. For, whilst time is so dealing with (1) and (2) that very few people now dispute them, the amount of our legitimate claim against Germany has not been brought into so sharp a focus by the pressure of events. Yet if my contention about this can be substantiated, the world will find it easier to arrange a practical settlement. The claims of justice in this connection are generally thought to be opposed to those of possibility, so that even if the pressure of events drives us reluctantly to admit that the latter must prevail, the former will rest unsatisfied. If, on the other hand, restricting ourselves to the devastations in France and Belgium, we can demonstrate that it is within the capacity of Germany to make full reparation, a harmony of sentiment and action can be established.

With this end in view it is necessary that I should take up again, in the light of the fuller information now available, the statements which I made in *The Economic Consequences of the Peace* [*JMK*, vol. II, 75] to the effect that 'the amount of the material damage done in the invaded districts has been the subject of enormous, if natural, exaggeration'. These statements have involved me in a charge, with which Frenchmen as eminent as M. Clemenceau[1] and M. Poincaré have associated themselves, that I was actuated not by the truth but by a supposed hostility

[1] It is of these passages that M. Clemenceau wrote as follows in his preface to M. Tardieu's book: 'Fort en thème d'économiste, M. Keynes (qui ne fut pas seul, dans la Conférence à professer cette opinion) combat, sans aucun ménagement, "l'abus des exigences des Alliés" (lisez: "de la France") et de ses négociateurs . . . Ces reproches et tant d'autres d'une violence brutale, dont je n'aurais rien dit, si l'auteur, à tous risques, n'eût cru servir sa cause en les livrant à la publicité, font assez clairement voir jusqu'où certains esprits

to France in speaking thus of the allegations of M. Klotz and M. Loucheur and some other Frenchmen. But I still urge on France that her cause may be served by accuracy and the avoidance of overstatement; that the damage she has suffered is more likely to be made good if the amount is possible than if it is impossible; and that, the more moderate her claims are, the more likely she is to win the support of the world in securing priority for them. M. Brenier, in particular, has conducted a widespread propaganda with the object of creating prejudice against my statistics. Yet to add a large number of noughts at the end of an estimate is not really an indication of nobility of mind. Nor, in the long run, are those persons good advocates of France's cause who bring her name into contempt and her sincerity into doubt by using figures wildly. We shall never get to work with the restoration of Europe unless we can bring not only experts, but the public, to consider coolly what material damage France has suffered and what material resources of reparation Germany commands. *The Times*, in a leading article which accompanied some articles by M. Brenier (4 December 1920), wrote with an air of noble contempt—'Mr Keynes treats their losses as matter for statistics'. But chaos and poverty will continue as long as we insist on treating statistics as an emotional barometer and as a convenient vehicle of sentiment. In the following examination of figures let us agree that we are employing them to measure facts and not as a literary expression of love or hate.

Leaving on one side for the present the items of pensions and allowances and loans to Belgium, let us examine the data relating to the material damage in Northern France. The claims made by the French government did not vary very much from the spring of 1919, when the Peace Conference was sitting, down to the spring of 1921, when the Reparation Commission was deciding its assessment, though the fluctuations in the value of the franc over that period cause some confusion. Early in 1919 M. Dubois,

s'étaient montés.' (In the English edition, M. Tardieu has caused the words *fort en thème d'économiste* to be translated by the words 'with some knowledge of economics but neither imagination nor character'—which seems rather a free rendering.)

speaking on behalf of the Budget Commission of the Chamber, gave the figure of 65 milliard francs 'as a minimum', and on 17 February 1919 M. Loucheur, speaking before the Senate as Minister of Industrial Reconstruction, estimated the cost at 75 milliards at the prices then prevailing. On 5 September 1919 M. Klotz, addressing the Chamber as Minister of Finance, put the total French claims for damage to property (presumably inclusive of losses at sea, etc.) at 134 milliards. In July 1920 M. Dubois, by that time President of the Reparation Commission, in a Report for the Brussels and Spa Conferences, put the figure at 62 milliards on the basis of pre-war prices.[1] In January 1921 M. Doumer, speaking as Finance Minister, put the figure at 110 milliards. The actual claim which the French government submitted to the Reparation Commission in April 1921 was for 127 milliard paper francs at current prices.[2] By that time the exchange value of the franc, and also its purchasing power, had considerably depreciated and, allowing for this, there is not so great a discrepancy as appears at first sight between the above estimates.

For the assessment of the Reparation Commission it was necessary to convert this claim from paper francs into gold marks. The rate to be adopted for this purpose was the subject of acute controversy. On the basis of the actual rate of exchange prevailing at that date (April 1921) the gold mark was worth about 3·25 paper francs. The French representatives claimed that this depreciation was temporary and that a permanent settlement ought not to be based on it. They asked, therefore, for a rate of about frs. 1·50 or frs. 1·75 to the gold mark.[3] The question was eventually submitted to the arbitration of Mr Boyden, the American member of the Reparation Commission who, like most

[1] At about the same date, the German Indemnity Commission (*Reichsentschädigungskommission*) estimated the cost at 7,228 million gold marks, also on the basis of pre-war prices; that is to say, at about one-seventh of M. Dubois' estimate.

[2] The details of this claim, so far as they have been published, are given in Appendix 3. The above figure comprises the items for industrial damages, damage to houses, furniture and fittings, unbuilt-on land, state property, and public works.

[3] See M. Loucheur's speech in the French Chamber, 20 May 1921.

arbitrators, took a middle course and decided that 2·20 paper francs should be deemed equivalent to 1 gold mark.[1] He would probably have found it difficult to give a reason for this decision. As regards that part of the claim which was in respect of pensions, a forecast of the gold value of the franc, however impracticable, was relevant. But as regards that part which was in respect of material damage, no such adjustment was necessary;[2] for the French claim had been drawn up on the basis of the current costs of reconstruction, the gold equivalent of which need not be expected to rise with an increase in the gold value of the franc, an improvement in the exchange being balanced sooner or later by a fall in franc prices. It might have been proper to make allowance for any premium existing at the date of the assessment, on the internal purchasing power of the franc over that of its external exchange-equivalent in gold. But in April 1921 the franc was not far from its proper 'purchasing power parity', and I calculate that on this basis it would have been approximately accurate to have equated the gold mark with 3 paper francs. The rate of 2·20 had the effect, therefore, of inflating the French claim against Germany very materially.

At this rate the claim of 127 milliard paper francs for material damage was equivalent to 57·7 milliard gold marks, of which the chief items were as follows:

|  | Francs (paper), millions | Marks (gold), millions |
|---|---|---|
| Industrial damages | 38,882 | 17,673 |
| Damage to houses | 36,892 | 16,768 |
| Furniture and fittings | 25,119 | 11,417 |
| Unbuilt-on land | 21,671 | 9,850 |
| State property | 1,958 | 890 |
| Public works | 2,583 | 1,174 |
| Total | 127,105 | 57,772 |

[1] For this rate to be justified the exchange value of the franc in New York must rise to about 11 cents.

[2] M. Loucheur's statement to the French Chamber implied that this rate of conversion was applicable to material damage as well as to pensions, and I have assumed this in what follows; but precise official information is lacking.

This total, equivalent to £2,886 million gold, is one which I believe to be a vast, indeed a fantastic, exaggeration beyond anything which it would be possible to justify under cross-examination. At the date when I wrote *The Economic Consequences of the Peace*, exact statistics as to the damage done were not available, and it was only possible to fix a maximum limit to a reasonable claim, having regard to the pre-war wealth of the invaded districts. Now, however, much more detail is available with which to check the claim.

The following particulars are quoted from a statement made by M. Briand in the French Senate on 6 April 1921, supplemented by an official memorandum published a few days later, and represent the position at about that date:[1]

(1) The population inhabiting the devastated districts in April 1921 was 4,100,000, as compared with 4,700,000 in 1914.

(2) Of the cultivable land 95 per cent of the surface had been relevelled and 90 per cent had been ploughed and was producing crops.

(3) 293,733 houses were totally destroyed, in replacement of

---

[1] The figures of damage done, given by M. Briand, are generally speaking rather lower than those given ten months earlier (in June 1920) in a report by M. Tardieu in his capacity as President of the Comité des Régions Dévastées. But the difference is not very material. For purposes of comparison, I give M. Tardieu's figures below together with those of the amount of reconstruction completed at that earlier date:

| | Destroyed | Repaired |
|---|---|---|
| Houses totally destroyed | 319,269 | 2,000 |
| Houses partially destroyed | 313,675 | 182,000 |
| Railway lines | 5,534 km. | 4,042 km. |
| Canals | 1,596 km. | 784 km. |
| Roads | 39,000 km. | 7,548 km. |
| Bridges, embankments, etc. | 4,785 km. | 3,424 km. |

| | Destroyed | Cleared from shells | Levelled | Ploughed |
|---|---|---|---|---|
| Arable land (hectares) | 3,200,000 | 2,900,000 | 1,700,000 | 1,150,000 |

| | Destroyed | Reconstructed and working | Under reconstruction |
|---|---|---|---|
| Factories and works | 11,500 | 3,540 | 3,812 |

A much earlier estimate is that made by M. Dubois for the Budget Commission of the French Chamber and published as Parliamentary Paper No. 5432 of the Session of 1918.

which 132,000 provisional dwellings of different kinds had been erected.

(4) 296,502 houses were partially destroyed, of which 281,000 had been repaired.

(5) Fifty per cent of the factories were again working.

(6) Out of 2,404 kilometres of railway destroyed, practically the whole had been reconstructed.

It seems, therefore, that, apart from refurnishing and from the rebuilding of houses and factories, the greater part of which had still to be accomplished, the bulk of the devastation was already made good out of the daily labour of France within two years of the Peace Conference, before Germany had paid anything.

This is a great achievement—one more demonstration of the riches accruing to France from the patient industry of peasants, which makes her one of the rich countries of the world, in spite of the corrupt Parisian finance which for a generation past has wasted the savings of her investors. When we look at Northern France we see what honest Frenchmen can accomplish.[1] But

---

[1] A more recent estimate (namely, for 1 July 1921) has been given, presumably from official sources, by M. Fournier-Sarlovèze, Deputy for the Oise. The following are some of his figures:

| INHABITED HOUSES | | | |
|---|---|---|---|
| At the Armistice | | By July 1921 | |
| totally destroyed | 289,147 | entirely rebuilt | 118,863 |
| badly injured | 164,317 | temporarily repaired | 182,694 |
| partially injured | 258,419 | | |

| PUBLIC BUILDINGS | | | | | |
|---|---|---|---|---|---|
| | Churches | Municipal buildings | Schools | Post offices | Hospitals |
| Destroyed | 1,407 | 1,415 | 2,243 | 171 | 30 |
| Damaged | 2,079 | 2,154 | 3,153 | 271 | 197 |
| Restored | 1,214 | 322 | 720 | 53 | 28 |
| Temporarily patched up | 1,097 | 931 | 2,093 | 196 | 128 |

| CULTIVATED LAND | | | |
|---|---|---|---|
| At the Armistice | Acres | By July 1921 | |
| totally destroyed | 4,693,516 | levelled | 4,067,408 |
| | | ploughed | 3,528,950 |

Footnote continued on p.75

when we turn to the money claims which are based on this, we are back in the atmosphere of Parisian finance—so grasping, faithless, and extravagantly unveracious as to defeat in the end its own objects.

For let us compare some of these items of devastation with the claims lodged.

(1) 293,733 houses were totally destroyed and 296,502 were partially destroyed. Since nearly all the latter have been repaired, we shall not be underestimating the damage in assuming, for the purposes of a rough comparison, that, on the average, the damaged houses were *half* destroyed, which gives us altogether the equivalent of 442,000 houses totally destroyed. Turning back, we find that the French Government's claim for damage to houses was 16,768 million gold marks, that is to say, £1,006 million.[1] Dividing this sum by the number of houses, we find an average claim of £2,275 per house![2] This is a claim for what were chiefly peasants' and miners' cottages and the tenements of small country towns. M. Tardieu has quoted M. Loucheur as saying that the houses in the Lens–Courrières district were worth 5,000 francs (£200) apiece before the war, but would cost 15,000 francs to rebuild after the war, which sounds not at all unreasonable. In April 1921 the cost of building construction in Paris (which had been a good deal higher some months before) was estimated to be, in terms of paper francs, three and a half times the pre-war figure.[3] But even if we take the cost in francs

| | LIVESTOCK | | |
| | 1914 | November 1918 | July 1921 |
|---|---|---|---|
| Cattle | 890,084 | 57,500 | 478,000 |
| Horses, donkeys, and mules | 412,730 | 32,600 | 235,400 |
| Sheep and goats | 958,308 | 69,100 | 276,700 |
| Pigs | 357,003 | 25,000 | 169,000 |

[1] Assuming an exchange of £1 = $4.
[2] Even if we assumed that every house which had been injured at all was totally destroyed, the figure would work out at about £1,700.
[3] M. Brenier, who has spent much time criticising me, quotes with approval (*The Times*, 24 January 1921) a French architect as estimating the cost of reconstruction at an average of £500 per house, and quotes also, without dissent, a German estimate that the pre-war

at five times the pre-war figure, namely 25,000 paper francs per house, the claim lodged by the French government is still three and a half times the truth. I fancy that the discrepancy, here and also under other heads, may be partly explained by the inclusion in the official French claim of indirect damages, namely, for loss of rent—*perte de loyer*. It does not appear what attitude the Reparation Commission took up towards *indirect* pecuniary and business losses arising in the devastated districts out of the war. But I do not think that such claims are admissible under the Treaty. Such losses, real though they were, were not essentially different from analogous losses occurring in other areas, and indeed throughout the territory of the Allies. The maximum claim, however, on this head would not go far towards justifying the above figure, and we can allow a considerable margin of error for such additional items without impairing the conclusion that the claim is exaggerated. In *The Economic Consequences of the Peace* [*JMK*, vol. II, 80] I estimated that £250 million (gold) might be a fair estimate for damage to house property; and I still think that this was about right.

(2) This claim for damage to houses is exclusive of furniture and fittings, which are the subject of a separate claim, namely, for 11,417 million gold marks, or nearly £700 million sterling. To check this figure let us assume that the whole of the furniture and fittings were destroyed, not only where the houses were destroyed, but also in every case where a house was damaged. This is an overstatement, but we may set it off against the fact that in a good many cases the furniture may have been looted and not recovered by restitution (a large amount has, in fact, been

average was £240. He also states, in the same article, that the number of houses destroyed was 304,191 and the number damaged 290,425, or 594,616 in all. Having pointed out the importance of not overlooking sentiment in these questions, he then multiplies £500, not by the number of houses but by the number of the *population*, and arrives at an answer of £750 million. What is one to reply to sentimental multiplication? What is the courteous retort to controversy on these lines? (His other figures are clearly such a mass of misprints, muddled arithmetic, confusion between hectares and acres and the like, that, whilst an attack could easily make a devastated area of them, it would be unfair to base any serious criticism on this well-intentioned farrago. As a writer on these topics, M. Brenier is about of the calibre of M. Raphäel-Georges Lévy.)

recovered in this way), although the structure of the house was not damaged at all. The total number of houses damaged or destroyed was 590,000. Dividing this into £700 million sterling, we have an average of £1,180 per house—an average valuation of the furniture and fittings in each peasant's or collier's house of more than £1,000! I hesitate to guess how great an overstatement shows itself here.

(3) The largest claim of all, however, is for 'industrial damages', namely, 17,673 million gold marks, or about £1,060 million sterling. In 1919 M. Loucheur estimated the cost of reconstruction of the coal-mines at 2,000 million francs, that is £80 million at the par of exchange.[1] As the pre-war value of all the coal-mines in Great Britain was estimated at only £130 million, and as the pre-war output of the British mines was fifteen times that of the invaded districts of France, this figure seems high.[2] But even if we accept it, there is still nearly a thousand millions sterling to account for. The great textile industries of Lille and Roubaix were robbed of their raw material, but their plant was not seriously injured, as is shown by the fact that in 1920 the woollen industry of these districts was already employing 93·8 per cent and the cotton industry 78·8 per cent of their pre-war personnel. At Tourcoing 55 factories out of 57 were in operation, and at Roubaix 46 out of 48.[3]

Altogether 11,500 industrial establishments are said to have been interfered with, but this includes every village workshop, and about three-quarters of them employed less than 20 persons. Half of them were at work again by the spring of 1921. What is the average claim made on their behalf? Deducting the coal-mines as above and dividing the total claim by 11,500, we reach

[1] M. Tardieu states that, on account of the subsequent rise in prices, M. Loucheur's estimate has proved, in terms of paper francs, to be inadequate. But this is allowed for by my having converted paper francs into sterling at the par of exchange.

[2] The Lens coal-mines, which were the object of most complete destruction, comprised 29 pits, and had, in 1913, 16,000 workmen with an output of 4 million tons.

[3] I take these figures from M. Tardieu, who argues, most illuminatingly, in alternate chapters, according to his thesis for the time being, that reconstruction has hardly begun, and that it is nearly finished.

an average figure of £8,500. The exaggeration seems *prima facie* on as high a scale as in the case of houses and furniture.

(4) The remaining item of importance is for unbuilt-on land. The claim under this head is for 9,850 million gold marks, or about £590 million sterling. M. Tardieu (*op. cit.* p. 347) quotes Mr Lloyd George as follows, in the course of a discussion during the Peace Conference in which he was pointing out the excessive character of the French claims: 'If you had to spend the money which you ask for the reconstruction of the devastated regions of the North of France, I assert that you could not manage to spend it. Besides, the land is still there. Although it has been badly upheaved in parts, it has not disappeared. Even if you put the Chemin des Dames up to auction, you would find buyers.' Mr Lloyd George's view has been justified by events. In April 1921 the French Prime Minister was able to tell his Senate that 95 per cent of the cultivable land had been re-levelled and that 90 per cent had been ploughed and was producing crops. Some go so far as to maintain that the fertility of the soil has been actually improved by the disturbance of its surface and by its lying fallow for several years. But apart from its having proved easier than was anticipated to make good this category of damage, the total cultivated area (excluding woodland) of the whole of the eleven Departments affected was about 6,650,000 acres, of which 270,000 acres were in the 'zone of destruction', 2 million acres in the 'zone of trenches and bombardment', and 4,200,000 acres in the 'zone of simple occupation'. The claim, therefore, averaged *over the whole area*, works out at about £90 per acre, and averaged over the first two categories above, at about £260 per acre. This claim, though it is described as being in respect of unbuilt-on land, probably includes farm buildings (other than houses), implements, livestock, and the growing crops of August 1914. As experience has proved that the permanent qualities of the land have only been seriously impaired over a small area, these latter items should probably constitute the major part of the claim. We have also to allow for destruction of woodlands. But

even with high estimates for each of these items, I do not see how we could reach a total above a third of the amount actually claimed.

These arguments are not exact, but they are sufficiently so to demonstrate that the claim sent in to the Reparation Commission is untenable. I believe that it is at least four times the truth. But it is possible that I have overlooked some items of claim, and it is better in discussions of this kind to leave a wide margin for possible error. I assert, therefore, that on the average the claim is not less than two or three times the truth.

I have spent much time over the French claim, because it is the largest, and because more particulars are available about it than about the claims of the other Allies. On the face of it, the Belgian claim is open to the same criticism as the French. But in this claim a larger part is played by levies on the civilian population and personal injuries to civilians. The material damage, however, was on a very much smaller scale than in France. Belgian industry is already working at its pre-war efficiency, and the amount of reconstruction still to be made good is not on a great scale. The Belgian Minister for Home Affairs stated in Parliament in February 1920 that at the date of the Armistice 80,000 houses and 1,100 public buildings had been destroyed. This suggests that the Belgian claim on this head ought to be about a quarter of the French claim; but in view of the greater wealth of the invaded districts of France, the Belgian loss is probably decidedly less than a quarter of the French loss. The claim, actually submitted by Belgium, for property, shipping, civilians and prisoners (that is to say, the aggregate claim apart from pensions and allowances), amounted to 34,254 million Belgian francs. Inasmuch as the Belgian Ministry of Finance, in an official survey published in 1913, estimate the entire wealth of the country at 29,525 million Belgian francs, it is evident that, even allowing for the diminished value of the Belgian franc, which is our measuring rod, this claim is very grossly excessive. I should guess that the degree of exaggeration is quite as great as in the case of France.

The British Empire claim is, apart from pensions and allowances, almost entirely in respect of shipping losses. The tonnage lost and damaged is definitely known. The value of the cargoes carried is a matter of difficult guesswork. On the basis of an average of £30 for the hull and £40 for the cargo per gross ton lost, I estimated the claim in *The Economic Consequences of the Peace* [*JMK*, vol. II, 83] at £540 million. The actual claim lodged was for £767 million. Much depends on the date at which the cost of replacement is calculated. Most of the tonnage was in fact replaced out of vessels the building of which commenced before the end of the war or shortly afterwards, and thus cost a much higher price than prevailed in, e.g., 1921. But even so the claim lodged is very high. It seems to be based on an estimate of £100 per gross ton lost for hull and cargo together, any excess in this being set off against the fact that no separate allowance is made for vessels damaged or molested, but not sunk. This figure is the highest for which any sort of plausible argument could be adduced, rather than a judicial estimate. I adhere to the estimate which I gave in *The Economic Consequences of the Peace*.

I forbear to examine the claims of the other Allies. The details, so far as they have been published, are given in Appendix 3.

The observations made above relate to the claims for material damage and do not bear on those for pensions and allowances, which are, nevertheless, a very large item. These latter are to be calculated, according to the Treaty, in the case of pensions 'as being the capitalised cost at the date of coming into force of the Treaty, on the basis of the scales in force in France at such date', and in the case of allowances made during hostilities to the dependants of mobilised persons 'on the basis of the average scale for such payments in force in France' during each year. That is to say, the French army scale is to be applied all round; and the result, given the numbers affected, should be a calculable figure, in which there should be little room for serious error. The actual claims were as follows in milliard gold marks:[1]

---

[1] Francs are here converted at 2·20 to the gold mark and the £ sterling at 1:20.

|  | Milliard marks (gold) |
|---|---|
| France | 33 |
| British Empire | 37 |
| Italy | 17 |
| Belgium | 1 |
| Japan | 1 |
| Roumania | 4 |
|  | 93 |

This does not include Serbia, for which a separate figure is not available, or the United States. The total would work out, therefore, at about 100 milliard gold marks.[1]

What does the aggregate of the claims work out at under all heads, and what relation does this total bear to the final assessment of the Reparation Commission? As the claims are stated in a variety of national currencies, it is not quite a simple matter to reach a total. In the following table French francs are converted into gold marks at 2·20 (the rate adopted by the Commission as explained above), sterling approximately at par (on the analogy of the rate for francs), Belgian francs at the same rate as French francs, Italian lire at twice this rate, Serbian dinars at four times this rate, and Japanese yen at par.

|  | Milliard marks (gold) |
|---|---|
| France | 99 |
| British Empire | 54 |
| Italy | 27 |
| Belgium | $16\frac{1}{2}$ |
| Japan | $1\frac{1}{2}$ |
| Jugoslavia | $9\frac{1}{2}$ |
| Roumania | 14 |
| Greece | 2 |
|  | $223\frac{1}{2}$ |

There are omitted from this table Poland and Czechoslovakia, of which the claims are probably inadmissible, the United States,

[1] This is exactly the figure of the estimate which I gave in *The Economic Consequences of the Peace* [*JMK* II, 101]. But I there added: 'I feel much more confidence in the approximate accuracy of the total figure than in its division between the different claimants.' This proviso was necessary, as I had over-estimated the claims of France and under-estimated those of the British Empire and of Italy.

which submitted no claim, and certain minor claimants shown in Appendix 3.

In round figures, therefore, we may put the claims as lodged before the Reparation Commission at about 225 milliard gold marks, of which 95 milliards was in respect of pensions and allowances, and 130 milliards for claims under other heads.

The Reparation Commission, in announcing its decision, did not particularise as between different claimants or as between different heads of claim, and merely stated a lump sum figure. Their figure was 132 milliards; that is to say, about 58 per cent of the sums claimed. This decision was in no way concerned with Germany's capacity to pay, and was simply an assessment, intended to be judicial, as to the sum justly due under the heads of claim established by the Treaty of Versailles.

The decision was unanimous, but only in face of sharp differences of opinion. It is not suitable or in accordance with decency to set up a body of interested representatives to give a judicial decision in their own case. This arrangement was an offspring of the assumption which runs through the Treaty that the Allies are incapable of doing wrong, or even of partiality.

Nothing has been published in England about the discussions which led up to this conclusion. But M. Poincaré, at one time President of the Reparation Commission and presumably well informed about its affairs, has lifted a corner of the veil in an article published in the *Revue des Deux Mondes* for 15 May 1921. He there divulges the fact that the final result was a compromise between the French and the British representatives, the latter of whom endeavoured to fix the figure at 104 milliards, and defended this adjudication with skilful and even passionate advocacy.[1]

When the decision of the Reparation Commission was first announced, and was found to abate so largely the claims lodged with it, I hailed it, led away a little perhaps by its very close

[1] 'Elle avait été le résultat d'un compromis assez pénible entre le délégué français, l'honorable M. Dubois, et le représentant anglais, Sir John Bradbury, depuis lors démissionnaire, qui voulait s'en tenir au chiffre de cent quatre milliards et qui avait défendu la thèse du gouvernement britannique avec une habileté passionnée.'

agreement with my own predictions, as a great triumph for justice in international affairs. So, in a measure, I still think it. The Reparation Commission went a considerable way in disavowing the veracity of the claims of the Allied governments. Indeed, their reduction of the claims for items other than pensions and allowances must have been very great, since the claims for pensions, being capable of more or less exact calculation,[1] can hardly have been subject to an initial error of anything approaching 42 per cent. If, for example, they reduced the claim for pensions and allowances from 95 to 80 milliards, they must have reduced the other claims from 130 milliards to 52 milliards, that is to say, by 60 per cent. Yet even so, on the data now available, I do not believe that their adjudication could be maintained before an impartial tribunal. The figure of 104 milliards, attributed by M. Poincaré to Sir John Bradbury, is probably the nearest we shall get to a strictly impartial assessment.

To complete our summary of the facts two particulars must be added. (1) The total, as assessed by the Reparation Commission, comprehends the total claim against Germany *and her allies*. It includes, that is to say, the damage done by the armies of Austria-Hungary, Turkey, and Bulgaria, as well as by those of Germany. Payments, if any, made by Germany's allies must, presumably, be deducted from the sum due. But Annex 1 of the reparation chapter of the Treaty of Versailles is so drafted as to render Germany liable for the whole amount. (2) This total is exclusive of the sum due under the Treaty for the reimbursement of sums lent to Belgium by her Allies during the war. At the date of the London Agreement (May 1921) Germany's liability under this head was provisionally estimated at 3 milliard gold marks. But it had not then been decided at what rate these loans, which were made in terms of dollars, sterling, and francs, should be converted into gold marks. The question was referred for

---

[1] The chief question of legitimate controversy in this connection was that of the rate of exchange for converting paper francs into gold marks.

arbitration to Mr Boyden, the United States delegate on the Reparation Commission, and at the end of September 1921 he announced his decision to the effect that the rate of conversion should be based on the rate of exchange prevailing at the date of the Armistice. Including interest at 5 per cent, as provided by the Treaty, I estimate that this liability amounts at the end of 1921 to about 6 milliard gold marks, of which slightly more than a third is due to Great Britain and slightly less than a third each to France and the United States respectively.

I take, therefore, as my final conclusion that the best available estimate of the sum due from Germany, under the strict letter of the Treaty of Versailles, is 110 milliard gold marks, which may be divided between the main categories of claim in the proportions—74 milliards for pensions and allowances, 30 milliards for direct damage to the property and persons of civilians, and 6 milliards for war debt incurred by Belgium.

This total is more than Germany can pay. But the claim exclusive of pensions and allowances may be within her capacity. The inclusion of a demand for pensions and allowances was the subject of a long struggle and a bitter controversy in Paris. I have argued that those were right who maintained that this demand was inconsistent with the terms on which Germany surrendered at the Armistice. I return to this subject in the next chapter.


## EXCURSUS 5

### RECEIPTS AND EXPENSES PRIOR TO 1 MAY 1921

The provision in the Treaty of Versailles that Germany, subject to certain deductions, was to pay £1,000 million (gold) before 1 May 1921, was so remarkably wide of facts and possibilities that for some time past no one has said much about this offspring of the unimaginative imaginations of Paris. As it was totally abandoned by the London Agreement of 5 May 1921, there is no need to return to what is an obsolete controversy. But it is interesting to record what payments Germany did actually effect during the transitional period.

The following details are from a statement published by the British Treasury in August 1921:

APPROXIMATE STATEMENT BY THE REPARATION COMMISSION OF DELIVERIES MADE BY GERMANY FROM 11 NOVEMBER 1918 TO 30 APRIL 1921

| | Gold marks |
|---|---|
| Receipts in cash | 99,334,000 |
| Deliveries in kind: | |
| Ships | 270,331,000 |
| Coal | 437,160,000 |
| Dyestuffs | 36,823,000 |
| Other deliveries | 937,040,000 |
| | 1,780,688,000 |
| Immovable property and assets not yet encashed | 2,754,104,000 |
| | 4,534,792,000 |
| say | £284,500,000 |

The immovable property consists chiefly of the Saar coalfields surrendered to France, state property in Schleswig surrendered to Denmark, and state property (with certain exceptions) in the territory transferred to Poland.

The whole of the cash, two-thirds of the ships, and a quarter of the dyestuffs accrued to Great Britain. A share of the ships and dyestuffs, the Saar coalfields, the bulk of the coal and of the 'other deliveries', including valuable materials left behind by the German army, accrued to France. Some ships, a proportion of the coal and other deliveries, and the compensation, payable by Denmark in respect of Schleswig, fell to Belgium. Italy obtained a portion of the coal and ships and some other trifles. The value of German state property in Poland could not be transferred to anyone but Poland.

But the sums thus received were not available for reparation. There had to be deducted from them (1) the sums returned to Germany under the Spa Agreement, namely 360 million gold marks,[1] and (2) the costs of the armies of occupation.

[1] Made up of about £5,500,000 advanced by Great Britain, 772 million francs by France, 96 million francs by Belgium, 147 million lire by Italy, and 56 million francs by Luxembourg.

In September 1921 the Reparation Commission published an approximate estimate, as follows, of the cost of occupation of German territory by the Allied armies from the Armistice until 1 May 1921:

|  | Total cost | Cost per man per day |
|---|---|---|
| United States | $278,067,610 | $4.50 |
| Great Britain | £52,881,298 | 14s |
| France | Frs. 2,304,850,470 | Frs. 15·25 |
| Belgium | Frs. 378,731,390 | Frs. 16·50 |
| Italy | Frs. 15,207,717 | Frs. 22 |

The conversion of these sums into gold marks raises the usual controversy as to the rates at which conversion is to be effected. The total was estimated, however, at three milliard gold marks,[1] of which one milliard was owed to the United States, one milliard to France, 900 million to Great Britain, 175 million to Belgium, and 5 million to Italy. On 1 May 1921 France had about 70,000 soldiers on the Rhine, Great Britain about 18,000, and the United States a trifling number.

The net result of the transitional period was, therefore, as follows:

(1) Putting on one side state property transferred to Poland, the whole of the transferable wealth obtained from Germany in the two and a half years following the Armistice under all the rigours of the Treaty, designed as they were to extract every available liquid asset, just about covered the costs of collection, that is to say, the expenses of the armies of occupation, and left *nothing* over for reparation.

(2) But as the United States has not yet been paid the milliard owing to her for her army, the other Allies have received between

---

[1] The German authorities have published a somewhat higher figure. According to a memorandum submitted to the Reichstag in September 1921 by their Finance Minister, the costs of the armies of occupation and the Rhine Provinces Commission up to the end of March 1921 were 3,936,954,542 gold marks, in respect of expenditure met in the first instance by the occupying Powers, and subsequently recoverable from Germany, *plus* 7,313,911,829 paper marks in respect of expenditure directly met by the German authorities.

them on balance a surplus of about one milliard. This surplus was not divided amongst them equally. Great Britain had received 450–500 million gold marks *less* than her expenses, Belgium 300–350 million *more* than her expenses, and France 1,000–1,200 million *more* than her expenses.[1]

Under the strict letter of the Treaty those Allies who had received less than their share might have claimed to be paid the difference in cash by those who had received more. This situation and the allocation of the milliard paid by Germany between May and August 1921 were the subject of the Financial Agreement provisionally signed at Paris on 13 August 1921. This Agreement chiefly consisted of concessions to France, partly by Belgium, who agreed in effect to a partial postponement of her priority charge on two milliards out of the first sums received from Germany for reparation, and partly by Great Britain, who accepted for the purposes of internal accounting amongst the Allies themselves a lower value for the coal delivered by Germany than the value fixed by the Treaty.[2] In view of these concessions about future payment, the *first* milliard in cash, received *after* 1 May 1921, was divided between Great Britain and Belgium, the former receiving 450 million gold marks in discharge of the balance still due to her in respect of the costs of occupation, and the balance falling to the latter as a further instalment of her agreed priority charge. This Agreement was represented in the French press as laying new burdens upon France, or at least as withdrawing existing rights from her. But this was not the case. The Agreement was directed throughout to moderating the harshness with which the letter of the Treaty and the arrangements of Spa would have operated against France.[3]

[1] I do not vouch for the accuracy of these figures, which are rough estimates of my own on the basis of incomplete published information.
[2] On the other hand, Great Britain's view was adopted as to the valuation of shipping.
[3] In view of the political difficulties in which this Agreement involved M. Briand's Cabinet, the matter was apparently adjusted by Great Britain and Belgium receiving their quotas as above, 'subject to adjustment of the final settlement' of the questions dealt with in the Agreement. The net result on 30 September 1921 was that, including the above sum, Great Britain had been repaid £5,445,000 in respect of the Spa coal advances, and had also received, or was in course of collecting, about £43 million towards the expenses of the

The actual value of these deliveries is a striking example of how far the value of deliverable articles falls below the estimates which used to be current. The Reparation Commission have stated that the credit which Germany will receive in respect of her mercantile marine will amount to about 755 million gold marks. This figure is low, partly because many of the ships were disposed of after the slump in tonnage.[1] Nevertheless, this was one of the tangible assets of great value, which it was customary at one time to invoke in answer to those who disputed Germany's capacity to make vast payments. What does it amount to in relation to the bill against her? The bill is 138 milliard gold marks, on which interest at 6 per cent for one year is 8,280 million gold marks. That is to say, Germany's mercantile marine in its entirety, of which the surrender humbled so much pride and engulfed so vast an effort, would about meet a month's charges.

## EXCURSUS 6

### THE DIVISION OF RECEIPTS AMONGST
### THE ALLIES

The Allied governments took advantage of the Spa meeting (July 1920) to settle amongst themselves a reparation question which had given much trouble in Paris and had been left unsolved,[2]— namely, the proportions in which the reparation receipts are to be divided between the various Allied claimants.[3] The Treaty provides that the receipts from Germany will be divided by the

army of occupation (approximately £50 million). Thus, as the result of three years' reparations, Great Britain's costs of collection had been about £7 million more than her receipts.

[1] To value these ships at what they fetched during the slump, yet to value Germany's liability for submarine destruction at what the ships cost to replace during the boom, appears to be unjust. My estimate (in *The Economic Consequences of the Peace* [*JMK*, vol. II, 110] of the value of the ships to be delivered was £120 million.

[2] M. Tardieu (*The Truth about the Treaty*, pp. 346–8) has given an account of the abortive discussion of this question at the Peace Conference. The French obtained at Spa a ratio very slightly *more* favourable to themselves than that which they had claimed and Mr Lloyd George had rejected at Paris.

[3] For a summary of the text of this Agreement see Appendix 1.

Allies 'in proportions which *have* been determined upon by them in advance, on a basis of general equity and of the rights of each'. The failure, described by M. Tardieu, to reach an agreement in Paris, rendered the tense of this provision inaccurate, but at Spa it was settled as follows:

| | |
|---|---|
| France | 52 per cent |
| British Empire[1] | 22 per cent |
| Italy | 10 per cent |
| Belgium | 8 per cent |
| Japan and Portugal | ¾ of 1 per cent each; |

the remaining 6½ per cent being reserved for the Serbo-Croat–Slovene state and for Greece, Roumania, and other Powers not signatories of the Spa Agreement.

This settlement represented some concession on the part of Great Britain, whose proportionate claim was greatly increased by the inclusion of pensions beyond what it would have been on the basis of reparation proper; and the proportion claimed by Mr Lloyd George in Paris was probably nearer the truth (namely, that the French and British shares should be in the proportion 5 to 3). I estimate that France 45 per cent, British Empire 33 per cent, Italy 10 per cent, Belgium 6 per cent, and the rest 6 per cent would have been more exactly in accordance with the claims of each under the Treaty. In view of all the facts, however, the Spa division may be held to have done substantial justice on the whole.

At the same time the priority to Belgium to the extent of £100 million (gold) was confirmed; and it was agreed that the loans made to Belgium during the war by the other Allies, for which

---

[1] At the conference of Dominion Prime Ministers in July 1921 this share was further divided as follows between the constituent portions of the Empire:

| | | | |
|---|---|---|---|
| United Kingdom | 86·85 | New Zealand | 1·75 |
| Minor colonies | 0·80 | South Africa | 0·60 |
| Canada | 4·35 | Newfoundland | 0·10 |
| Australia | 4·35 | India | 1·20 |

[2] The Spa Agreement also made provision that half the receipts from Bulgaria and from the constituent parts of the former Austro-Hungarian Empire should be divided in the above proportions, and that, of the other half, 40 per cent should go to Italy and 60 per cent to Greece, Roumania, and Jugoslavia.

Germany is liable under Article 232[1] of the Treaty, should be dealt with out of the moneys next received. These loans, including interest, will amount by the end of 1921 to something in the neighbourhood of £300 million (gold), of which £110 million will be due to Great Britain, £100 million to France, and £90 million to the United States.

Under the Spa Agreement, therefore, sums received from Germany in cash, and credits in respect of deliveries in kind, were to be applied to the discharge of her obligations in the following order:

1. The cost of the armies of occupation, estimated at £150 million (gold) up to 1 May 1921.

2. Advances to Germany for food purchases under the Spa Agreement, say £18 million (gold).

3. Belgian priority of £100 million (gold).

4. Repayment of allied advances to Belgium, say £300 million (gold).

This amounts to about £570 million (gold) altogether, of which I estimate that about £150 million (gold) is due to France, £170 million (gold) to Great Britain, £110 million (gold) to Belgium, and £140 million (gold) to the United States.

Very few people, I think, have appreciated how large a sum is due to the United States under the strict letter of the Agreement. Since France has already received almost two-thirds of her share as above, whilst Belgium has had about one-third, Great Britain less than one-third, and the United States nothing, it follows that, even on the most favourable hypothesis as to Germany's impending payments, comparatively small sums are strictly due to France in the near future.

The Financial Agreement of 13 August 1921 was aimed at modifying the harshness of these priority provisions towards

---

[1] 'Germany undertakes ... to make reimbursement of all sums which Belgium has borrowed from the Allies and Associated Governments up to 11 November 1918, together with interest at the rate of 5 per cent per annum on such sums.' The priority for this repayment arranged at Spa is a little different from the procedure contemplated in the Treaty, which provided for repayment not later than 1 May 1926.

France.[1] The details of this Agreement have not yet been published, but it is said to make a somewhat different provision from that contemplated at Spa for the repayment of Allied war advances to Belgium.

The reception of this Agreement by the French public was a good illustration of the effect of keeping people in the dark. The effect of the Spa Agreement had never been understood in France, with the result that the August Financial Agreement, which much improved France's position, was believed to interfere seriously with her existing rights. M. Doumer never had the pluck to tell his public the truth, although, if he had, it would have been clear that, in signing the Agreement provisionally, he was acting in the interests of his country.

The mention of the United States invites attention to the anomalous position of that country under the Peace Treaty. Her failure to ratify the Treaty forfeits none of her rights under it, either in respect of her share of the costs of the army of occupation (which, however, is offset to a small extent by the German ships she has retained), or in respect of the repayment of her war advances to Belgium.[2] It follows that the United States is entitled, on the strict letter, to a considerable part of the cash receipts from Germany in the near future.

There is, however, a possible offset to these claims which has been mentioned already (p. 50) but must not be overlooked here. Under the Treaty private German property in an Allied country is, in the case of countries adopting the Clearing House Scheme, applied in the first instance to debts owing from German nationals to the nationals of the Allied country in question, and the balance, if any, is retained for reparation. What is to happen

---

[1] See above, p. 87.

[2] Article 1 of the Treaty of Peace between Germany and the United States, signed on 25 August 1921, and since ratified, expressly stipulates that Germany undertakes to accord to the United States all the rights, privileges, indemnities, reparations, and advantages specified in the joint resolution of Congress of 2 July 1921, 'Including all the rights and advantages stipulated for the benefit of the United States under the Treaty of Versailles which the United States shall enjoy notwithstanding the fact that such Treaty has not been ratified by the United States.'

in the case of similar German assets in the United States is still undetermined. The surplus assets, the value of which may be about $300 million,[1] will be retained, until Congress determines otherwise, by the Enemy Property Custodian. There have been negotiations from time to time for a loan in favour of Germany on the security of these assets, but the legal position has rendered progress impossible. At any rate this important German asset is still under American control.

[1] According to a statement published in Washington in August 1921 the Custodian had in his hands German property to the value of $314,179,463.

# Chapter 5

# THE LEGALITY OF THE
# CLAIM FOR PENSIONS

*The application of morals to international politics is more a thing to be desired than a thing which has been in operation. Also, when I am made a participant in crime along with many millions of other people, I more or less shrug my shoulders.—Letter from a friendly critic to the author of* The Economic Consequences of the Peace.

We have seen in the preceding chapter that the claim for pensions and allowances is nearly double that for devastation, so that its inclusion in the Allies' demands nearly trebles the bill. It makes the difference between a demand which can be met and a demand which cannot be met. Therefore it is important.

In *The Economic Consequences of the Peace* I gave reasons for the opinion that this claim was contrary to our engagements and an act of international immorality. A good deal has been written about it since then, but I cannot admit that my conclusion has been seriously disputed. Most American writers accept it; most French writers ignore it; and most English writers try to show, not that the *balance* of evidence is against me, but that there are a few just plausible, or just not-negligible, observations to be made on the other side. Their contention is that of the Jesuit professors of probabilism in the seventeenth century, namely, that the Allies are justified unless it is absolutely certain that they are wrong, and that any probability in their favour, however small, is enough to save them from mortal sin.

But most people in the countries of Germany's former enemies are not ready to excite themselves very much, even if my view is accepted. The passage at the head of this chapter describes a common attitude. International politics is a scoundrel's game and always has been, and the private citizen can scarcely feel himself personally responsible. If our enemy breaks the rules, his action may furnish us with an appropriate opportunity for expressing our feelings; but this must not be taken to commit us to a cool opinion that such things have never happened before and must never happen again. Sensitive and honourable patriots do not like it, but they 'more or less shrug' their shoulders.

There is some common sense in this. I cannot deny it. International morality, interpreted as a crude legalism, might be very injurious to the world. It is at least as true of these vast-scale transactions, as of private affairs, that we judge wrongly if we do not take into account *everything*. And it is superficial to appeal, the other way round, to the principles which do duty when propaganda is blistering herd emotion with its brew of passion, sentiment, self-interest, and moral fiddlesticks.

But whilst I see that nothing rare has happened and that men's motives are much as usual, I do still think that this particular act was an exceptionally mean one, made worse by hypocritical professions of moral purpose. My object in returning to it is partly historical and partly practical. New material of high interest is available to instruct us about the course of events. And if for practical reasons we can agree to drop this claim, we shall make a settlement easier.

Those who think that it was contrary to the Allies' engagements to charge pensions against the enemy base this opinion on the terms notified to the German government by President Wilson, with the authority of the Allies, on 5 November 1918, subject to which Germany accepted the Armistice conditions.[1] The contrary opinion that the Allies were fully entitled to charge pensions if they considered it expedient to do so, has been supported by two distinct lines of argument: first that the Armistice conditions

---

[1] I have given the exact text of the relevant passages in *The Economic Consequences of the Peace*, chapter 5.

of 11 November 1918 were not *subject* to President Wilson's notification of 5 November 1918, but *superseded* it, more particularly regarding reparation; and alternatively that the wording of President Wilson's notification properly understood does not exclude pensions.

The first line of argument was adopted by M. Klotz and the French government during the Peace Conference, and has been approved more recently by M. Tardieu.[1] It was repudiated by the whole of the American delegation at Paris, and never definitely supported by the British government. Responsible writers about the Treaty, other than French, have not admitted it.[2] It was also explicitly abandoned by the Peace Conference itself in its reply to the German observations on the first draft of the Treaty. The second line of argument was that of the British government during the Peace Conference, and it was an argument on these lines which finally converted President Wilson. I will deal with the two arguments in turn.

1. Various persons have published particulars, formerly confidential, which allow us to reconstruct the course of the discussions about the Armistice. These begin with the examination of the Armistice terms by the Allied Council of War on 1 November 1918.[3]

---

[1] *The Truth about the Treaty*, p. 208.

[2] E.g. *The History of the Peace Conference of Paris*, published under the auspices of the Institute of International Affairs, delivers judgement as follows (II, 43): 'It is this statement then (i.e. President Wilson's notification of 5 November 1918) which must be taken as the ruling document in any discussion as to what the Allies were entitled to claim by way of reparation in the Treaty of Peace, and it is difficult to interpret it otherwise than as a deliberate limitation of their undoubted right to recover the whole of their war costs.'

[3] The following particulars are taken from *Les Négociations secrètes et les Quatre Armistices avec pièces justificatives* by 'Mermeix', published at Paris by Ollendorff, 1921. This remarkable volume has not received the attention it deserves. The greater part of it consists of a verbatim transcript of the secret *procès verbaux* of those meetings of the Supreme Council of the Allies which were concerned with the Armistice terms. On the face of it this disclosure is authentic and is corroborated in part by M. Tardieu. There are many passages of extraordinary interest on points not connected with my present topic, as for example the discussion of the question whether the Allies should insist on the surrender of the German fleet if the Germans made trouble about it. Marshal Foch emerges from this record very honourably, as determined that nothing unnecessary should be demanded of the enemy, and that no blood should be spilt for a vain or trifling object. Sir Douglas Haig was of the same opinion. In reply to Col. House, Foch spoke thus: 'If they accept the terms of the Armistice we are imposing on them, it is a capitulation. Such a capitulation

The first point which emerges is that the reply of the Allied governments to President Wilson (which afterwards furnished the text of his notification of 5 November 1918, addressed to Germany), defining their interpretation of the references to reparation in the Fourteen Points, was drawn up and approved at the *same* session of the Supreme Council (that of 1, 2 November) which drew up the relevant clauses of the Armistice terms; and that the Allies did not finally approve the reply to President Wilson until *after* they had approved that very draft of the Armistice terms which, according to the French contention, superseded and negatived the terms outlined in the reply to President Wilson.[1]

The record of the proceedings of the Supreme Council (as now disclosed) lends no support to the existence in their minds of the duplicity which the French contention attributes to them. On the other hand, it makes it clear that the Council did not intend the references to reparation in the Armistice terms to modify in any way their reply to the President.

The record, in so far as it is relevant to this point, may be summarised as follows:[2] M. Clemenceau called attention to the absence of any reference in the first draft of the Armistice terms to the restitution of stolen property or to reparation. Mr Lloyd George replied that there ought to be some reference to restitution, but that reparation was a Peace condition rather than an Armistice condition. M. Hymans agreed with Mr Lloyd George.

gives us everything we could get from the greatest victory. In such circumstances I cannot admit that I have the right to risk the life of a single man more.' And again on 31 October: 'If our conditions are accepted we can wish for nothing better. We make war only to attain our ends, and we do not want to prolong it uselessly.' In reply to a proposal by Mr Balfour that the Germans in evacuating the East should leave one-third of their arms behind them, Foch observed: 'The intrusion of all these clauses makes our document chimerical, since the greater part of the conditions are incapable of being executed. We should do well to be sparing with these unrealisable injunctions.' Towards Austria also he was humane and feared the prolongation of the blockade which the politicians were proposing. 'I intervene', he said on 31 October 1918, 'in a matter which is not a military one strictly speaking. We are to maintain the blockade until Peace, that is to say until we have made a new Austria. That may take a long time; which means a country condemned to famine and perhaps impelled to anarchy.'

[1] This is corroborated by M. Tardieu, *op. cit.* p. 71.
[2] See Mermeix, *op. cit.* pp. 226–50.

MM. Sonnino and Orlando went further and thought that neither had any place in the Armistice terms, but were ready to accept the Lloyd George–Hymans compromise of including restitution but not reparation. The discussion was postponed for M. Hymans to draft a formula. On its resumption next day, it was M. Clemenceau who produced a formula consisting of the three words *Réparation des dommages*. M. Hymans, M. Sonnino, and Mr Bonar Law all expressed doubt whether this was in place in the Armistice terms. M. Clemenceau replied that he only wanted to mention the principle, and that French public opinion would be surprised if there was no reference to it. Mr Bonar Law objected: 'It is already mentioned in our letter to President Wilson which he is about to communicate to Germany. It is useless to repeat it.'[1] This observation met with no contradiction, but it was agreed on sentimental grounds and for the satisfaction of public opinion to add M. Clemenceau's three words. The Council then passed on to other topics. At the last moment, as they were about to disperse, M. Klotz slipped in the words: 'It would be prudent to put at the head of the financial questions a clause reserving the future claims of the Allies, and I propose to you the wording "Without prejudice to any subsequent claims and demands on the part of the Allies."'[2] It does not seem to have occurred to any of those present that this text could be deemed of material importance or otherwise than as protecting the Allies from the risk of being held to have surrendered any existing claims through failure to mention them in this document; and it was accepted without discussion. M. Klotz afterwards boasted that by this little device he had abolished the Fourteen Points, so far as they affected reparation and finance (although the very same meeting of the Allies had despatched a Note to President Wilson accepting them), and had secured to the

---

[1] This very important remark by Mr Bonar Law is also quoted by M. Tardieu (*op. cit.* p. 70) and is therefore of undoubted authenticity.

[2] 'Il serait prudent de mettre en tête des questions financières une clause réservant les revendications futures des Alliés et je vous propose le texte suivant: "Sous réserve de toutes revendications et réclamations ultérieures de la part des Alliés."'

Allies the right to demand from Germany the whole cost of the war. But I think the world will decide that the Supreme Council was right in attaching to these words no particular importance. Personal pride in so smart a trick has led M. Klotz, and his colleague M. Tardieu, to persist too long with a contention which decent persons have now abandoned.

There was an episode which has lately come to light connected with this passage which may be recounted as illustrating the pitfalls of the world. As M. Klotz only introduced his form of words as the Council was breaking up, it is likely that no undue attention was concentrated on it. But ill-fortune may dog anyone, and the same state of affairs seems to have led to one of the scribes getting the words down wrong. Instead of *revendication*, which means *demand*, the word *renonciation*, which means *concession*, got written in the text handed to the Germans for signature.[1] This word was not so suitable. But M. Klotz suffered less inconvenience from this mistake than might have been expected, since at the Peace Conference no one noticed that the French text of the Armistice Agreement as officially circulated, which M. Klotz used in arguing before the Reparation Committee, agreed in its wording with what he had intended it to be and not with the text which Germany had actually signed. Nevertheless it is the word *renonciation* which is still to be found in the official texts of the British and German governments.[2]

2. The other line of argument raises more subtle intellectual issues and is not a mere matter of prestidigitation. If it be granted that our rights are governed by the terms of the Note

[1] That is to say, this text ran, 'Sous réserve de toute renonciation et réclamation ultérieure', instead of 'Sous réserve de toutes revendications et réclamations ultérieures'.

[2] I record this episode as an historical curiosity. In my opinion it makes no material difference to the argument whether the text runs 'revendications et réclamations' or 'renonciation et réclamation'; for I regard either form of words as merely a protective phrase. But the plausibility of M. Klotz's position is decidedly weakened (if so weak a case is capable of further weakening) if it is the latter phrase which is authentic. The editor of the Institute of International Affairs' *History of the Peace Conference of Paris*, who was the first to discover and publish the discrepancy in question (v, 370–2), takes the view that the question of which text is used makes a material difference to the value of M. Klotz's argument.

addressed to Germany by President Wilson in the name of the Allies on 5 November 1918, the question depends on the interpretation of these terms. As Mr Baruch and M. Tardieu have now published between them the greater part of the official reports (including very secret documents) bearing on the discussion of this problem during the Peace Conference, we are in a better position than before to assess the value of the Allies' case.

The pronouncements by the President which were to form the basis of peace provided that there should be 'no contributions' and 'no punitive damages', but the invaded territories of Belgium, France, Roumania, Serbia, and Montenegro were to be restored. This did not cover losses from submarines or from air raids. Accordingly the Allied governments, when they accepted the President's formulas, embodied a reservation, on the point as to what 'restoration' covered, in the following sentence: 'By *it* (i.e. restoration of invaded territory) they understand that compensation will be made by Germany for all damage done to the civilian population of the Allies and to their property by the aggression of Germany by land, by sea, and from the air.'

The natural meaning and object of these words, which, the reader must remember, are introduced as an interpretation of the phrase 'restoration of invaded territory', is to assimilate submarine and cruiser aggression by sea and aeroplane and airship aggression by air to military aggression by land, which, in all the circumstances, was a reasonable extension of the phrase, provided it was duly notified beforehand. The Allies rightly apprehended that, if they accepted the phrase as it stood, 'restoration of invaded territory' might be limited to damage resulting from military aggression by land.

This interpretation of the reservation of the Allied governments, namely, that it assimilated offensive action by sea or air to offensive action by land, but that 'restoration of invaded territory' could not possibly include pensions and separation allowances, was adopted by the American delegation at Paris. They construed the German liability to be in respect of the 'direct physical damage to property of non-military character and direct physical injury to civilians'[1] caused by such aggression; the only further liability which they admitted being under a different part of the President's pronouncements, namely, those relating to breaches of international law, such as the breach of the Treaty of Neutrality in favour of Belgium, and the illegal treatment of prisoners of war.

I doubt if anyone would ever have challenged this interpretation if the British Prime Minister had not won a General Election by promises to extract from Germany more than this interpretation could justify,[2] and if the French government also had not raised unjustifiable expectations. These promises were made recklessly. But it was not easy for their authors to admit, so soon after they had been given, that they were contrary to our engagements.

The discussion opened with the delegations, other than the American, claiming that we had not committed ourselves to anything which precluded our demanding from Germany all the loss and damage, direct and indirect, which had resulted from the war. 'One of the Allies', says Mr Baruch, 'went even further, and made claim for loss and damage resulting from the fact that the Armistice was concluded so unexpectedly that the termination of hostilities involved it in financial losses.'

Various arguments were employed in the early stages, the British delegates to the Reparation Committee of the Peace Conference, namely, Mr Hughes, Lord Sumner and Lord Cunliffe, supporting the demand for complete war costs and not merely reparation for damage. They urged (1) that one of the principles enunciated by President Wilson was that each item of the Treaty should be just, and that it was in accordance with the general principles of justice to throw on Germany the whole

[1] Baruch, *op. cit.* p. 19.
[2] As Mr Baruch puts it (*op. cit.* p. 4): 'At an election held *after the Armistice and agreement as to the basic terms of peace*, the English people, by an overwhelming majority, returned to power their Prime Minister *on the basis of an increase in the severity of these terms of the peace*, especially those of reparation.' (The italics are mine.)

costs of the war; and (2) that Great Britain's war costs had resulted from Germany's breach of the Treaty of Neutrality of Belgium, and that therefore Great Britain (but not necessarily, on this argument, all the other Allies) was entitled to complete repayment in accordance with the general principles of international law. These general arguments were, I think, overwhelmed by the speeches made on behalf of the American delegates by Mr John Foster Dulles. The following are extracts from what he said:

If it is in accordance with our sentiment that the principles of reparation be severe, and in accord with our material interest that these principles be all inclusive, why, in defiance of these motives, have we proposed reparation in certain limited ways only? It is because, gentlemen, we do not regard ourselves as free. We are not here to consider as a novel proposal what reparation the enemy should in justice pay; we have not before us a blank page upon which we are free to write what we will. We have before us a page, it is true; but one which is already filled with writing, and at the bottom are the signatures of Mr Wilson, of Mr Orlando, of M. Clemenceau, and of Mr Lloyd George. You are all aware, I am sure, of the writing to which I refer: it is the agreed basis of peace with Germany.

Mr Dulles then recapitulated the relevant passages and continued:

Can there be any question that this agreement does constitute a limitation? It is perfectly obvious that it was recognised at the time of the negotiations in October and November 1918 that the reparation then specified for would limit the Associated Governments as to the reparation which they could demand of the enemy as a condition of peace. The whole purpose of Germany was to ascertain the maximum which would be demanded of her in the terms of peace, and the action of the Allies in especially stipulating at that time for an enlargement of the original proposal respecting reparation is explicable only on the theory that it was understood that once an agreement was concluded they would no longer be free to specify the reparation which Germany must make. We have thus agreed that we would give Germany peace if she would do certain specified things. Is it now open to us to say, 'Yes, but before you get peace you must do other and further things'? We have said to Germany, 'You may have peace if among other things you perform certain acts of reparation which will cost you, say, ten million dollars.' Are we not now clearly precluded from saying, 'You can have peace provided you perform other acts of reparation which will bring your total liability to many times that which was originally stipulated'? No; irrespective of the justice of the enemy making the latter reparation, it is now too late. Our bargain has been struck for better or for worse; it remains only to give it a fair construction and practical application.

It is a shameful memory that the British delegates never withdrew their full demands, to which they were still adhering when, in March 1921, the question was taken out of their hands by the Supreme Council. The American delegation cabled to the President, who was then at sea, for support in maintaining their position, to which he replied that the American delegation should dissent, and if necessary dissent publicly, from a procedure which 'is clearly inconsistent with what we deliberately led the enemy to expect and cannot now honourably alter simply because we have the power'.[1]

After this the discussions entered on a new phase. The British and French Prime Ministers abandoned the contentions of their delegates, admitted the binding force of the words contained in their Note of 5 November 1918, and settled down to extract some meaning from these words which would compose their differences and satisfy their constituents. What constituted 'damage done to the civilian population'? Could not this be made to cover military pensions and the separation allowances which had been made to the civilian dependants of soldiers? If so, the bill against Germany could be raised to a high enough figure to satisfy nearly everyone. It was pointed out, however, as Mr Baruch records, 'that financial loss resulting from the absence of a wage-earner did not cause any more "damage to the civilian population" than did an equal financial loss involved in the payment of taxes to provide military equipment and like war costs'. In fact, a separation allowance or a pension was simply one of many general charges on the Exchequer arising out of the costs of the war. If such charges were to be admitted as civilian

[1] Baruch, *op. cit.* p. 25.

damage, it was a very short step back to the claim for the entire costs of the war, on the ground that these costs must fall on the taxpayer who, generally speaking, was a civilian. The sophistry of the argument became exposed by pushing it to its logical conclusion. Nor was it clear how pensions and allowances could be covered by words which were themselves an interpretation of the phrase 'restoration of invaded territory'. And the President's conscience, though very desirous by now to be converted (for he had on hand other controversies with his colleagues which interested him more than this one), remained unconvinced.

The American delegates have recorded that the final argument which overbore the last scruples of the President was contained in a Memorandum prepared by General Smuts[1] on 31 March 1919. Briefly, this argument was, that a soldier becomes a civilian again after his discharge, and that, therefore, a wound, the effects of which persist after he has left the Army, is damage done to a civilian.[2] This is the argument by which 'damage done to the civilian population' came to include damage done to soldiers. *This* is the argument on which, in the end, our case was

---

[1] This Memorandum, which has been published *in extenso* by Mr Baruch (*op. cit.* pp. 29 seq.), belonged to the category of most secret documents. It has been given to the world by itself without the accompanying circumstances which, without justifying its arguments (on which indeed no further light could be thrown beyond what we already have in the narrative of Mr Baruch), might yet throw light on individual motives. I agree with the comment made by *The Economist* (22 October 1921) in reviewing vol. v of the *History of the Peace Conference of Paris* (published under the auspices of the Institute of International Affairs), which has reprinted this Memorandum, that 'a very serious injustice will be done to the reputation of General Smuts if this document continues to be reproduced and circulated without any explanation of the circumstances in which it was prepared'. Nevertheless it is well that the world should have this document, and it must take its place in a story which is more important to the world than the motives and reputations of individual actors in it.

[2] The following is the salient passage of the Memorandum: 'After the soldier's discharge as unfit he rejoins the civilian population, and as for the future he cannot (in whole or in part) earn his own livelihood, he is suffering damage as a member of the civilian population, for which the German Government are again liable to make compensation. In other words, the pension for disablement which he draws from the French Government is really a liability of the German Government, which they must under the above reservation make good to the French Government. It could not be argued that as he was disabled while a soldier he does not suffer damage as a civilian after his discharge if he is unfit to do his ordinary work. He does literally suffer as a civilian after his discharge, and his pension is intended to make good this damage, and is therefore a liability of the German Government.'

based! For at this straw the President's conscience clutched, and the matter was settled.

It had been settled in the privacy of the Four. I will give the final scene in the words of Mr Lamont, one of the American delegates:[1]

I well remember the day upon which President Wilson determined to support the inclusion of pensions in the Reparation Bill. Some of us were gathered in his library in the Place des États-Unis, having been summoned by him to discuss this particular question of pensions. We explained to him that we couldn't find a single lawyer in the American Delegation that would give an opinion in favour of including pensions. All the logic was against it. 'Logic! logic!' exclaimed the President, 'I don't care a damn for logic. I am going to include pensions!'[2]

Well! perhaps I was too near these things at the time and have become touched in the emotions, but I cannot 'more or less shrug my shoulders'. Whether or not that is the appropriate gesture, I have here set forth, for the inspection of Englishmen and our Allies, the moral basis on which two-thirds of our claims against Germany rest.

[1] *What Really Happened at Paris*, p. 272.
[2] Mr Lamont adds that 'it was not a contempt of logic, but simply an impatience of technicality; a determination to brush aside verbiage and get at the root of things. There was not one of us in the room whose heart did not beat with a like feeling.' These words not merely reflect a little naïvely the modern opportunist's impatience of legality and respect for the *fait accompli*, but also recall the atmosphere of exhaustion and the longing of everyone to be finished, somehow, with this dreadful controversy, which for months had outraged at the same time the intellects and the consciences of most of the participators. Yet, even so, to their lasting credit, the American Delegation had stood firm for the law, and it was the President, and he alone, who capitulated to the lying exigencies of politics.

Chapter 6

# REPARATION, INTER-ALLY DEBT, AND INTERNATIONAL TRADE

It is fashionable at the present time to urge a reduction of the Allies' claims on Germany and of America's claims on the Allies, on the ground that, as such payments can only be made in goods, insistence on these claims will be positively injurious to the claimants.

That it is in the self-interest of the Allies and of America to abate their respective demands, I hold to be true. But it is better not to use bad arguments, and the suggestion that it is necessarily injurious to receive goods for nothing is not plausible or correct. I seek in this chapter to disentangle the true from the false in the now popular belief that there is something harmful in compelling Germany to 'fling goods at us'.

The argument is a little intricate and the reader must be patient.

1. It does not make very much difference whether the debtor country pays by sending goods direct to the creditor or by selling them elsewhere and remitting cash. In either case the goods come on to the world market and are sold competitively or co-operatively in relation to the industries of the creditor, as the case may be, this distinction depending on the nature of the goods rather than on the market in which they are sold.

2. It is not much use to *earmark* non-competitive goods against the payment of the debt, so long as competitive goods are being sold by the debtor country in some other connection, e.g. to pay for its own imports. This is simply to bury one's head in the sand. For example, out of the aggregate of goods which Germany would naturally export in the event of her exports being forcibly stimulated, it might be possible to pick out a selection of non-

competitive goods; but it would not affect the situation in the slightest degree to pretend that it was these particular goods, and not the others, which were paying the debt. It is therefore useless to prescribe that Germany shall pay in certain specified commodities if these are commodities which she would export in any case, and useless, equally, to forbid her to pay in certain specified commodities, if that merely means that she will export these commodities to some other market to pay for her imports generally. No expedient on our part for making Germany pay us, or on America's part for making us pay her, in the shape of particular commodities affects the position, except in so far as it modifies the form of the paying country's exports *as a whole*.

3. On the other hand, it does us no harm to receive for nothing the proceeds of goods, even when they are sold competitively, if these goods would be sold on the world's market in any case.

4. If the result of pressing the debtor country to pay is to cause it to offer competitive goods at a lower price than it would otherwise, the particular industries in the creditor country which produce these goods are bound to suffer, even though there are balancing advantages for the creditor country as a whole.

5. In so far as the payments made by the debtor country accrue, not to the country with which the debtor's goods are competing, but to a third party, clearly there are no balancing advantages to offset the direct disadvantages under 4.

6. The answer to the question, whether the balancing advantages to the creditor country as a whole outweigh the injury to particular industries within that country, depends on the length of the period over which the creditor country can reasonably expect to go on receiving the payments. At first the injury to the industries which suffer from the competition and to those employed in them is likely to outweigh the benefit of the payments received. But, as in the course of time the capital and labour are absorbed in other directions, a balance of advantage may accrue.

The application of these general principles to the particular case of ourselves and Germany is easy. Germany's exports are so preponderantly competitive with ours that, if her exports are forcibly stimulated, it is certain that she will have to sell goods

| German exports | Percentage of total exports | | |
|---|---|---|---|
| | 1913 | 1920 (Jan.–Sept.) | 1921 (June–Sept.) |
| Iron and steel goods | 13·2 | 20 | 22 |
| Machinery (including motor cars) | 7·5 | 12 | 17 |
| Chemicals and dyes | 4 | 13 | 9·5 |
| Fuel | 7 | 6·5 | ? |
| Paper goods | 2·5 | 4 | 3·5 |
| Electrical goods | 2 | 3·5 | ? |
| Silk goods | 2 | 3 | |
| Cotton goods | 5·5 | 3 | 15 |
| Woollen goods | 6 | — | |
| Glass | 0·5 | 2·5 | 2 |
| Leather goods | 3 | 2 | 4 |
| Copper goods | 1·5 | 1·5 | ? |

against us. This is not altered by the fact that it is possible to pick out a few exports or potential exports, such as potash or sugar, which are not competitive. If Germany is to have a *large* surplus of exports over imports, she must increase her competitive sales. In *The Economic Consequences of the Peace* [*JMK*, vol. II, 119–25] I demonstrated this at some length on the basis of pre-war statistics. I showed that not only the goods she must sell, but the markets she must sell them in, were largely competitive with our own. The statistics of post-war trade show that the former argument still holds good. The table above shows the proportions in which her export trade was divided between the principal articles of export, (1) in 1913, (2) in the first nine months of 1920 (the latest period for which I have figures in this precise form), and (3) in the four months June to September 1921, these last figures representing, I think, a not exactly comparable classification, and being provisional only.

It is clear, therefore, that, though raw materials other than coal, such as potash, sugar, and timber, may yield a trifle,

Germany can only compass an export trade of great value by exporting iron and steel goods, chemicals, dyes, textiles, and coal, for these are the only export articles of which she can produce great quantities. It is also clear that there have been no very marked changes in the proportionate importance of the different export trades since the war, except that the exchange position has somewhat stimulated, relatively to the others, those export lines, such as iron goods, machinery, chemicals, dyes, and glass, which do not involve much importation of raw materials.

To compel Germany to pay a large indemnity is therefore the same thing as to compel her to expand some or all of the above-mentioned exports to a greater extent than she would do otherwise. The only way in which she can effect this expansion is by offering the goods at a lower price than that at which other countries care to offer them; putting herself in a position to offer them cheap, partly by the German working classes lowering their standard of life without reducing their efficiency in the same degree, and partly by German *export* industries being subsidised, directly or indirectly, at the expense of the rest of the community.

These facts, formerly overlooked, are now, perhaps, exaggerated by popular opinion. For principle 3, enunciated above, requires attention. Our industries will be subjected to strong competition from Germany, just as they were before the war, whether we exact reparation or not; and we must not ascribe to the reparation policy inconveniences which would exist in any case. The remedy lies not in the now popular nostrums for prescribing the *form* in which Germany shall pay, but in reducing the aggregate *amount* to a reasonable figure. For by prescribing the manner in which she shall pay *us* we do not control the form of her export trade as a whole; and by absorbing for reparation purposes the whole of a particular type of export, we compel her to expand her other exports to pay for her imports and other international obligations. On the other hand, we can secure from her moderate payments, on the sort of scale, for example, on which she might have been building up new foreign investments, without stimulating her exports as a whole to a greater activity than they would enjoy otherwise. This is the correct course for Great Britain from the standpoint of her own self-interest only.

The practical application of principles 5 and 6 is also clear. So far as 5 is concerned, Great Britain is to receive not the whole of the indemnity, but about a fifth of it; whilst 6 provides the argument which to me has always appeared decisive. The *permanence* of reparation payments on a large scale for a long period of years is, to say the least, not to be reckoned on. Who believes that the Allies will, over a period of one or two generations, exert adequate force over the German government, or that the German government can exert adequate authority over its subjects, to extract continuing fruits on a vast scale from forced labour? No one believes it in his heart; no one at all. There is not the faintest possibility of our persisting with this affair to the end. But if this is so, then, most certainly, it will not be worth our while to disorder our export trades and disturb the equilibrium of our industry for two or three years; much less to endanger the peace of Europe.

The same principles apply with one modification to the United States and to the exaction by her of the debts which the Allied governments owe. The industries of the United States would suffer, not so much from the competition of cheap goods from the Allies in their endeavours to pay their debts, as from the inability of the Allies to purchase from America their usual proportion of her exports. The Allies would have to find the money to pay America, not so much by selling more as by buying less. The farmers of the United States would suffer more than the manufacturers; if only because increased imports can be kept out by a tariff, whilst there is no such easy way of stimulating diminished exports. It is, however, a curious fact that whilst Wall Street and the manufacturing East are prepared to consider a modification of the debts, the Middle West and South is reported (I write ignorantly) to be dead against it. For two years

Germany was not required to pay cash to the Allies, and during that period the manufacturers of Great Britain were quite blind to what the consequences would be to themselves when the payments actually began. The Allies have not yet been required to begin to pay cash to the United States, and the farmers of the latter are still as blind as were the British manufacturers to the injuries they will suffer if the Allies ever try seriously to pay in full. I recommend Senators and Congressmen from the agricultural districts of the United States, lest they soon suffer the same moral and intellectual ignominy as our own high-reparation men, to invest at once in a little caution in their opposition to the efforts of Mr Harding's Administration to secure for itself a free hand to act wisely in this matter (and even perhaps generously) in accordance with the progress of opinion and of events.

The decisive argument, however, for the United States, as for Great Britain, is not the damage to particular interests (which would diminish with time), but the unlikelihood of permanence in the exaction of the debts, even if they were paid for a short period. I say this, not only because I doubt the ability of the European Allies to pay, but because of the great difficulty of the problem which the United States has before her in any case in balancing her commercial account with the Old World.

American economists have examined somewhat carefully the statistical measure of the change from the pre-war position. According to their estimates, America is now owed more interest on foreign investments than is due from her, quite apart from the interest on the debts of the Allied governments; and her mercantile marine now earns from foreigners more than she owes them for similar services. Her excess of exports of commodities over imports approaches $3,000 million a year;[1] whilst, on the other side of the balance, payments, mainly to Europe, in respect of tourists and of immigrant remittances are estimated at

---

[1] In the year of boom to June 1920, on a total trade of $13,350 million, the excess of exports over imports was $2,870 million. In the year, partly one of depression, to June 1921, on a total trade of $10,150 million, the excess of exports was $2,860 million.

not above $1,000 million a year. Thus, in order to balance the account as it now stands, the United States must lend to the rest of the world, in one shape or another, not less than $2,000 million a year, to which interest and sinking fund on the European governmental war debts would, if they were paid, add about $600 million.

Recently, therefore, the United States must have been lending to the rest of the world, mainly Europe, something like $2,000 million a year. Fortunately for Europe, a fair proportion of this was by way of speculative purchases of depreciated paper currencies. From 1919 to 1921 the losses of American speculators fed Europe; but this source of income can scarcely be reckoned on permanently. For a time the policy of loans can meet the situation; but, as the interest on past loans mounts up, it must in the long run aggravate it.

Mercantile nations have always employed large funds in overseas trade. But the practice of foreign investment, as we know it now, is a very modern contrivance, a very unstable one, and only suited to peculiar circumstances. An old country can in this way develop a new one at a time when the latter could not possibly do so with its own resources alone; the arrangement may be mutually advantageous, and out of abundant profits the lender may hope to be repaid. But the position cannot be reversed. If European bonds are issued in America on the analogy of the American bonds issued in Europe during the nineteenth century, the analogy will be a false one; because, taken in the aggregate, there is no natural increase, no *real* sinking fund, out of which they can be repaid. The interest will be furnished out of new loans, so long as these are obtainable, and the financial structure will mount always higher, until it is not worth while to maintain any longer the illusion that it has foundations. The unwillingness of American investors to buy European bonds is based on common sense.

At the end of 1919 I advocated (in *The Economic Consequences of the Peace*) a reconstruction loan from America to Europe, conditioned, however, on Europe's putting her own house in order. In the past two years America, in spite of European complaints to the contrary, has, in fact, made *very large* loans, much larger than the sum I contemplated, though not mainly in the form of regular, dollar-bond issues. No particular conditions were attached to these loans, and much of the money has been lost. Though wasted in part, they have helped Europe through the critical days of the post-Armistice period. But a continuance of them cannot provide a solution for the existing dis-equilibrium in the balance of indebtedness.

In part the adjustment may be effected by the United States taking the place hitherto held by England, France, and (on a small scale) Germany in providing capital for those new parts of the world less developed than herself—the British Dominions and South America. The Russian Empire, too, in Europe and Asia, is to be regarded as virgin soil, which may at a later date provide a suitable outlet for foreign capital. The American investor will lend more wisely to these countries, on the lines on which British and French investors used to lend to them, than direct to the old countries of Europe. But it is not likely that the whole gap can be bridged thus. Ultimately, and probably soon, there must be a readjustment of the balance of exports and imports. America must buy more and sell less. This is the only alternative to her making to Europe an annual present. Either American prices must rise faster than European (which will be the case if the Federal Reserve Board allows the gold influx to produce its natural consequences), or, failing this, the same result must be brought about by a further depreciation of the European exchanges, until Europe, by inability to buy, has reduced her purchases to articles of necessity. At first the American exporter, unable to scrap all at once the processes of production for export, may meet the situation by lowering his prices; but when these have continued, say for two years, below his cost of production, he will be driven inevitably to curtail or abandon his business.

It is useless for the United States to suppose that an equilibrium position can be reached on the basis of her exporting at least as much as at present, and at the same time restricting her imports by a tariff. Just as the Allies demand vast payments from Germany, and then exercise their ingenuity to prevent her paying them, so the American Administration devises, with one hand, schemes for financing exports and, with the other, tariffs which will make it as difficult as possible for such credits to be repaid. Great nations can often act with a degree of folly which we should not excuse in an individual.

By the shipment to the United States of all the bullion in the world, and the erection there of a sky-scraping golden calf, a short postponement may be gained. But a point may even come when the United States will refuse gold, yet still demand to be paid—a new Midas vainly asking more succulent fare than the barren metal of her own contract.

In any case the readjustment will be severe, and injurious to important interests. If, in addition, the United States exacts payment of the Allied debts, the position will be intolerable. If she persevered to the bitter end, scrapped her export industries and diverted to other uses the capital now employed in them, and if her former European associates decided to meet their obligations at whatever cost to themselves, I do not deny that the final result might be to America's material interest. But the project is utterly chimerical. It will not happen. Nothing is more certain than that America will not pursue such a policy to its conclusion; she will abandon it as soon as she experiences its first consequences. Nor, if she did, would the Allies pay the money. The position is exactly parallel to that of German reparation. America will not carry through to a conclusion the collection of Allied debt, any more than the Allies will carry through the collection of their present reparation demands. Neither, in the long run, is serious politics. Nearly all well-informed persons admit this in private conversation. But we live in a curious age when utterances in the press are deliberately designed to be in conformity with the worst-informed, instead of with the best-informed, opinion, because the former is the wider spread; so that for comparatively long periods there can be discrepancies, laughable or monstrous, between the written and the spoken word.

If this is so, it is not good business for America to embitter her relations with Europe, and to disorder her export industries for two years, in pursuance of a policy which she is certain to abandon before it has profited her.

For the benefit of any reader who enjoys an abstract statement, I summarise the argument thus. The equilibrium of international trade is based on a complicated balance between the agriculture and the industries of the different countries of the world, and on a specialisation by each in the employment of its labour and its capital. If one country is required to transfer to another without payment great quantities of goods, for which this equilibrium does not allow, the balance is destroyed. Since capital and labour are fixed and organised in certain employments and cannot flow freely into others, the disturbance of the balance is destructive to the utility of the capital and labour thus fixed. The *organisation*, on which the wealth of the modern world so largely depends, suffers injury. In course of time a new organisation and a new equilibrium can be established. But if the origin of the disturbance is of temporary duration, the losses from the injury done to organisation may outweigh the profit of receiving goods without paying for them. Moreover, since the losses will be concentrated on the capital and labour employed in particular industries, they will provoke an outcry out of proportion to the injury inflicted on the community as a whole.

Chapter 7

# THE REVISION OF THE TREATY
# AND THE
# SETTLEMENT OF EUROPE

*Shylock.* I'll have my bond; I will not hear thee speak:
I'll have my bond; and therefore speak no more.

The deeper and the fouler the bogs into which Mr Lloyd George leads us, the more credit is his for getting us out. He leads us in to satisfy our desires; he leads us out to save our souls. He hands us down the primrose path and puts out the bonfire just in time. Who, ever before, enjoyed the best of heaven and hell as we do?

In England, opinion has nearly completed its swing, and the Prime Minister is making ready to win a General Election on Forbidding Germany to Pay, Employment for Everyone, and a Happier Europe for All. Why not, indeed? But this Faustus of ours shakes too quickly his kaleidoscope of haloes and hellfire, for me to depict the hues as they melt into one another. I shall do better to construct an independent solution, which is *possible* in the sense that nothing but a change in the popular will is necessary to achieve it, hoping to influence this will a little, but leaving it to those whose business it is to gauge the moment at which it will be safe to embroider such patterns on a political banner.

If I look back two years and read again what I wrote then, I see that perils which were ahead are now passed safely. The patience of the common people of Europe and the stability of its institutions have survived the worst shocks they will receive. Two years ago the Treaty, which outraged justice, mercy, and wisdom, represented the momentary will of the victorious countries. Would the victims be patient? Or would they be driven by despair and privation to shake society's foundations? We have the answer now. They have been patient. Nothing very much has happened, except pain and injury to individuals. The communities of Europe are settling down to a new equilibrium. We are almost ready to turn our minds from the avoidance of calamity to the renewal of health.

There have been other influences besides that patience of the common people which often before has helped Europe through worse evils. The actions of those in power have been wiser than their words. It is only a slight exaggeration to say that no parts of the Peace Treaties have been carried out, except those relating to frontiers and to disarmament. Many of the misfortunes which I predicted as attendant on the execution of the reparation chapter have not occurred, because no serious attempt has been made to execute it. And, whilst no one can predict with what particular sauce the makers of the Treaty will eat their words, there can no longer be any question of the actual enforcement of this chapter. And there has been a third factor, not quite in accordance with expectations, paradoxical at first sight, but natural, nevertheless, and concordant with past experience—the fact that it is in times of growing profits and not in times of growing distress that the working classes stir themselves and threaten their masters. When times are bad and poverty presses on them they sink back again into a weary acquiescence. Great Britain and all Europe have learnt this in 1921. Was not the French Revolution rather due perhaps to the growing wealth of eighteenth-century France—for at that time France was the richest country in the world—than to the pressure of taxation or the exactions of the old régime? It is the profiteer, not privation, that makes man shake his chains.

In spite, therefore, of trade depression and disordered exchanges, Europe, under the surface, is much stabler and much healthier than two years ago. The disturbance of minds is less. The organisation, destroyed by war, has been partly restored; transport, except in Eastern Europe, is largely repaired; there has been a good harvest, everywhere but in Russia, and raw materials are abundant. Great Britain and the United States and their markets overseas have suffered a cyclical fluctuation of trade prosperity of a greater amplitude than ever before; but there are indications that the worst point is passed.

Two obstacles remain. The Treaty, though unexecuted, is not revised. And that part of organisation which consists in currency regulation, public finance, and the foreign exchanges, remains nearly as bad as it ever was. In most European countries there is still no proper balance between the expenditure of the state and its income, so that inflation continues and the international values of their currencies are fluctuating and uncertain. The suggestions which follow are mainly directed towards these problems.

Some contemporary plans for the reconstruction of Europe err in being too paternal or too complicated; also, sometimes, in being too pessimistic. The patients need neither drugs nor surgery, but healthy and natural surroundings in which they can exert their own recuperative powers. Therefore a good plan must be in the main *negative*; it must consist in getting rid of shackles, in simplifying the situation, in cancelling futile but injurious entanglements. At present everyone is faced by obligations which they cannot meet. Until the problem set to the finance ministers of Europe is a *possible* one, there can be little incentive to energy or to the exercise of skill. But if the situation was made such that an insolvent country could have only itself to blame, then the highest integrity and the most accomplished financial technique would, in each separate country, have its chance. I seek by the proposals of this chapter, not to prescribe a solution, but to create a situation in which a solution is possible.

In their main substance, therefore, my suggestions are not novel. The now familiar project of the cancellation, in part or in their entirety, of the reparation and inter-allied debts, is a large and unavoidable feature of them. But those who are not prepared for these measures must not pretend to a serious interest in the reconstruction of Europe.

In so far as such cancellation or abatement involves concessions by Great Britain, an Englishman can write without embarrassment and with some knowledge of the tendency of popular opinion in his own country. But where concessions by the United States are concerned he is in more difficulty. The attitude of a section of the American press furnishes an almost irresistible temptation to deal out the sort of humbug (or discrete half-truths) which are believed to promote cordiality between nations; it is easy and terribly respectable; and, what is much worse, it may even do good where frankness would do harm. I pursue the opposite course, with a doubting and uneasy conscience, yet supported (not only in this chapter but throughout my book) by the hope, possibly superstitious, that openness does good in the long run, even when it makes trouble at first.

So far, reparation on a large scale has not been collected from Germany. So far, the Allies have not paid interest to the United States on what they owe. Our present troubles, when they are not attributable to the after-effects of war and the cyclical depression of trade, are due, therefore, not to the enforcement of these claims, but to the uncertainties of their possible enforcement. It follows, therefore, that merely to put off the problem will do us no good. That is what we have been doing for two years already. Even to reduce our reparation demands to Germany's maximum actual capacity and really force her to pay them, might make matters worse than they are. To write down inter-ally debts by half and then try to collect them, would be an aggravation, not a cure, of the existing difficulties. The solution, therefore, must not be one which tries to extract the last theoretical penny from everybody; its main object must be to set the finance ministers of *every* country a problem not incapable of wise solution over the next five years.

## I. THE REVISION OF THE TREATY

The Reparation Commission have assessed the Treaty claims at 138 milliard gold marks, of which 132 milliards are for pensions and damage and 6 milliards for Belgian debt. They have not stated in what proportions the 132 milliards are divided between pensions and damages. My own assessment of the Treaty claims (p. 84 above) is 110 milliards, of which 74 milliards are for pensions and allowances, 30 milliards for damage, and 6 milliards for Belgian debt.

The arguments of chapter 6 make it incumbent on those who are convinced by them to abandon as dishonourable the claims to pensions and allowances. This reduces the claims to 36 milliards, a sum which it may not be in our interest to exact in full, but which is probably within Germany's theoretical capacity to pay.

Apart from clearing out of the way various clauses which are no longer operative or useful, and from terminating the occupation on conditions set forth below, I should limit my Revision of the Treaty to this simple stroke of the pen. Let the present assessment of 138 milliard gold marks be replaced by 36 milliard gold marks.

We are strictly entitled under the Armistice terms to these 36 milliards; and if prudence recommends an abatement below that figure, such abatement can properly be made, on terms, by those and those only who are entitled to the claims. I estimate with some confidence that this sum of 36 milliards is divisible between the Allies about in the proportions shown in the table on the following page.

The payment by Germany of 5 per cent interest and 1 per cent sinking fund on this total sum is not, in my judgement, theoretically impossible. But it could only be done by stimulating her export industries in a manner injurious and irritating to Great Britain, and by imposing on her Treasury a financial problem of such difficulty that it would tend to unsound finance and to weak,

|  | Damage | Belgian debt | Total |
|---|---|---|---|
| British Empire | 9 | 2 | 11 |
| France | 16 | 2 | 18 |
| Belgium | 3 | — | 3 |
| Italy | 1 | — | 1 |
| United States | — | 2 | 2 |
| Others | 1 | — | 1 |
|  | 30 | 6 | 36 |

unstable governments. Even though this payment is theoretically possible, I do not think that it is practically obtainable over a period of thirty years.

I recommend therefore that as a separate arrangement from the Revision of the Treaty as above, the British Empire should waive the whole of their claims, with the exception of 1 milliard gold marks reserved for a special purpose explained below, and should undertake to square the claims of Italy and the minor claimants by cancellation of debt owing from them; thus leaving Germany to pay 18 milliards to France and 3 milliards to Belgium (on the assumption that the United States also would forgo the trifle due to her). This sum should be discharged by an annual payment of 6 per cent of the sum due (being 5 per cent interest and 1 per cent sinking fund) over a period of thirty years. With the assistance of minor measures to ease the opening period, it is reasonable to suppose that this amount could be paid without serious injury to anyone.

In so far as it proves convenient to discharge this liability in goods, and not in cash, so much the better. But I see no advantage in laying stress on this. It would be wiser to leave Germany to find the money as best she can, any payment in goods being by mutual agreement, as in the Wiesbaden plan.

It may lead, however, to great anomalies to fix the annual payments in terms of *gold* over so long a period as thirty years. If gold prices fall, the burden may become intolerable. If gold prices rise, the claimants may be cheated of their expectations. The annual payment should be adjusted, therefore, by some impartial authority, with reference to an index number of the commodity-value of gold.

The other Treaty change relates to the occupation. It would promote peaceable relations in Europe if, as a part of the new settlement, the Allied troops were withdrawn altogether from German territory, and all rights of invasion for whatever purpose waived, except by leave of a majority vote of the League of Nations. But in return the British Empire and the United States should guarantee to France and Belgium all reasonable assistance, short of warfare, in securing satisfaction for their reduced claims; whilst Germany should guarantee the complete de-militarisation of her territory west of the Rhine.

## II. THE SATISFACTION OF THE ALLIES

*France.* Is it in the interest of France to accept this settlement? If it is combined with further concessions from Great Britain and the United States by the cancellation of her debts to them, it is overwhelmingly in her interest.

What is her present balance sheet of claims and liabilities? She is entitled to 52 per cent of what Germany pays. On p. 48 I have calculated what this will be under the London Settlement, (*a*) on the basis of German exports at the rate of 6 milliards, namely 3·56 milliard gold marks; and (*b*) on the basis of exports at the rate of 10 milliards, namely 4·60 milliard gold marks. France's share, therefore, is 1·85 milliards per annum on assumption (*a*), and 2·39 milliards on assumption (*b*). On the other hand, she owes the United States $3,634 million and the United Kingdom £557 million. If these sums be converted into gold marks at par, and the annual charge on them is calculated at 5 per cent for interest and 1 per cent for sinking fund, her liability is 1·48 milliards per annum. That is to say, if Germany pays in full and if the more favourable assumption (*b*) is adopted as to the growth of her exports, the most for which France can hope under existing arrangements is a net sum of 0·91 milliard gold marks (£45,500,000 gold) per annum. Whereas under the revised scheme she will not only be entitled to a greater sum, namely 1·08 milliard gold marks (£54 million gold) per annum; but, inasmuch as she will be accorded a priority on Germany's available resources, and as the total charge is within Germany's capacity, she may reasonably expect to be paid.

My proposal provides for the complete restoration of the devastated provinces at a fair valuation of the actual damage done, and it abandons other rival claims which stand in the way of the priority of this paramount claim. But apart from this, about which opinions will differ, and apart from the increased likelihood which it affords of really getting payment, France will actually receive a larger sum than if the letter of the existing agreements is adhered to all round.

*Belgium* is entitled at present to 8 per cent of the receipts, which under the London Settlement would amount to 280 million gold marks per annum on assumption (*a*) and 368 million on assumption (*b*). Under the new proposal she will receive 180 million gold marks per annum and will gain in certainty what she loses in possible receipts. The satisfaction of her existing priority should be adjusted by mutual agreement between herself and France.

*Italy* would gain immensely. She is entitled to 10 per cent of the receipts under the London Settlement (together with some claims on problematical receipts from Austria and Bulgaria); that is to say, 326 million gold marks per annum on assumption (*a*) and 460 million on assumption (*b*). But these sums are far below the annual charge of her obligations towards the United Kingdom and the United States which, converted into gold marks on the same basis as that employed above in the case of France, amounts to 1,000 million gold marks per annum.

### III. THE ASSISTANCE OF NEW STATES

I have reserved above, out of the claims of Great Britain, a sum of 1 milliard gold marks, with the object, not that she should retain this sum for herself, but that she should use it to ease the financial problems of two states for which she has a certain responsibility, namely Austria and Poland.

*Austria*'s problems are well known and attract a general sympathy. The Viennese were not made for tragedy; the world feels that, and there is none so bitter as to wish ill to the city of Mozart. Vienna has been the capital of degenerate greatness but, released from imperial temptations, she is now free to fulfil her true rôle of providing for a quarter-part of Europe the capital of commerce and the arts. Somehow she has laughed and cried her way through the last two years; and now, I think, though on the surface her plight is more desperate than before, a very little help will be enough. She has no army, and by virtue of the depreciation of her money a trifling internal debt. Too much help may make of her a lifelong beggar; but a little will raise her from despondency and render her financial problem no longer beyond solution.

My proposal, then, is to cancel the debts she owes to foreign governments, including empty claims to reparation, and to give her a comparatively small sum out of the milliard gold marks reserved from British claims on Germany. Credits placed at her disposal in Berlin, equivalent in value to 300 million gold marks, to be available, as required, over a period of five years, might be enough.

For the other new States, the cancellation of debt owing and, in the case of Hungary, of reparation claims, should be enough, except for Poland.

*Poland*, too, must be acknowledged to be a possible problem, but it is not easy to be practical with so impracticable a subject. Her main problem can be solved only by time, and the recovery of her neighbours. I deal here only with the urgent question of making just possible for her a reorganisation of currency, and of facilitating a peaceable intercourse between herself and Germany. For this purpose I would assign to her the balance of the reserved milliard, namely, 700 million gold marks, of which the annual interest should be available to her unconditionally, but of which the capital should be employed only for a currency reorganisation, under conditions to be approved by the United States and Great Britain.

In its essentials this scheme is very simple. I think that it satisfies my criterion of leaving every finance minister in Europe with a possible problem. The rest must come gradually, and I will not burden the argument of this book by considering along what lines the detailed solutions should be sought.

Who are the losers? Even on paper—far more in reality—every continental country gains an advantage. But on paper the United States and the United Kingdom are losers. What is each of them giving up?

Under the London Settlement Great Britain is entitled to 22 per cent of the receipts, which is from 780 to 1,010 million gold marks per annum (£39 million to £50,500,000 gold) according to which assumption is adopted as to the volume of German exports. She is owed by various European governments (including Russia, see Appendix 9) £1,800 million, which at 6 per cent for interest and sinking fund is £108 million per annum. On paper she would forgo these sums, say £150 million per annum, altogether. In actual fact, her prospects of securing more than a fraction of this amount are remote. Great Britain lives by commerce, and most Englishmen now need but little persuading that she will gain more in honour, prestige, and wealth by employing a prudent generosity to preserve the equilibrium of commerce and the well-being of Europe, than by attempting to exact a hateful and crushing tribute, whether from her victorious Allies or her defeated enemy.

The United States would forgo on paper a capital sum of about 6,500 million dollars which, at 6 per cent, represents an annual charge of $390 million (£78 million gold). But in my opinion the chance of her being actually paid any considerable amount of this, if she tries to exact it, is decidedly remote.[1] Is there any likelihood of the United States joining in such a scheme *soon enough* (for I feel confident she will cancel these debts in the end) to be useful?

Most Americans with whom I have discussed this question express themselves as personally favourable to the cancellation of the European debts, but add that so great a majority of their countrymen think otherwise that such a proposal is at present outside practical politics. They think, therefore, that it is premature to discuss it; for the present, America must pretend she is going to demand the money and Europe must pretend she is going to pay it. Indeed, the position is much the same as that of German reparation in England in the middle of 1921. Doubtless my informants are right about this public opinion, the mysterious entity which is the same thing perhaps as Rousseau's General Will. Yet, all the same, I do not attach to what they tell me too much importance. Public opinion held that Hans Andersen's Emperor wore a fine suit; and in the United States especially, public opinion changes sometimes, as it were, *en bloc*.

If, indeed, public opinion were an unalterable thing, it would be a waste of time to discuss public affairs. And though it may be the chief business of newsmen and politicians to ascertain its momentary features, a writer ought to be concerned, rather, with what public opinion should be. I record these platitudes because many Americans give their advice, as though it were actually immoral to make suggestions which public opinion does not now approve. In America, I gather, an act of this kind is considered so reckless, that some improper motive is at once suspected, and criticism takes the form of an inquiry into the culprit's personal character and antecedents.

[1] This scheme is in no way concerned with the debt of Great Britain to the United States which is excluded from the above figures. The question of the right treatment of this debt (which differs from the others chiefly because the interest on it is capable of being actually collected in cash) raises other issues with which I am not dealing here. The above proposals for cancellation relate solely to the debts owing by the governments of continental Europe to the governments of Great Britain and the United States.

Let us inquire, however, a little more deeply into the sentiments and emotions which underlie the American attitude to the European debts. They want to be generous to Europe, both out of good feeling and because many of them now suspect that any other course would upset their own economic equilibrium. But they don't want to be 'done'. They do not want it to be said that once again the old cynics in Europe have been one too many for them. Times, too, have been bad and taxation oppressive; and many parts of America do not feel rich enough at the moment to favour a light abandonment of a possible asset. Moreover, these arrangements between nations warring together they liken much more closely than we do to ordinary business transactions between individuals. It is, they say, as though a bank having made an unsecured advance to a client in whom they believe, at a difficult time when he would have gone under without it, this client were then to cry off paying. To permit such a thing would be to do an injury to the elementary principles of business honour.

The average American, I fancy, would like to see the European nations approaching him with a pathetic light in their eyes and the cash in their hands, saying, 'America, we owe to you our liberty and our life; here we bring what we can in grateful thanks, money not wrung by grievous taxation from the widow and orphan, but saved, the best fruits of victory, out of the abolition of armaments, militarism, Empire, and internal strife, made possible by the help you freely gave us.' And then the average American would reply: 'I honour you for your integrity. It is what I expected. But I did not enter the war for profit or to invest my money well. I have had my reward in the words you have just uttered. The loans are forgiven. Return to your homes and use the resources I release to uplift the poor and the unfortunate.' And it would be an essential part of the little scene that his reply should come as a complete and overwhelming surprise.

Alas for the wickedness of the world! It is not in international affairs that we can secure the sentimental satisfactions which we all love. For only individuals are good, and all nations are dishonourable, cruel, and designing. In deciding whether Italy (for example) must pay what she owes, America must consider the consequences of trying to make her pay—so far as self-interest is concerned, in terms of economic equilibrium between America and Italy and, so far as generosity is concerned, in terms of Italian peasants and their lives. And whilst the various prime ministers will telegraph something suitable, drafted by their private secretaries, to the effect that America's action makes the moment of writing the most important in the history of the world and proves that Americans are the noblest creatures living, America must not expect adequate or appropriate thanks.

Nevertheless, since time presses, we cannot rely on American assistance, and we must do without it if necessary. If America does not feel ready to participate in a conference of revision and reconstruction, Great Britain should be prepared to do her part in the cancellation of paper claims, irrespective of similar action by the United States.

The simplicity of my plan may be emphasised by summarising it. (1) Great Britain, and if possible America too, to cancel all the debts owing them from the governments of Europe and to waive their claims to any share of German reparation; (2) Germany to pay 1,260 million gold marks (£63 million gold) per annum for 30 years, and to hold available a lump sum of 1,000 million gold marks for assistance to Poland and Austria; (3) this annual payment to be assigned in the shares 1,080 million gold marks to France and 180 million to Belgium.

This would be a just, sensible, and permanent settlement. If France were to refuse it, she would indeed be sacrificing the substance to the shadow. In spite of superficial appearances to the contrary, it is also in the self-interest of Great Britain. Perhaps British public opinion, profoundly altered though it now is, may not yet be reconciled to obtaining nothing. But this is a case where a wise nation will do best by acting in a large way. I have not neglected to consider with care the various possible devices by which Great Britain might get, or appear to get, something for herself from the settlement. She might take, for instance, in satisfaction of her claims some of the C bonds under the London Settlement which, having a third priority after provision for the A and B bonds, can be given a nominal value but are really worth nothing. She might, in lieu of receiving a share of the proceeds of the German customs, stipulate that her goods should be admitted into Germany free of duty. She might seek a partial control over German industries, or obtain the services of German organisation for the future exploitation of Russia. Plans of this sort attract an ingenious mind and are not to be discarded too hastily. Yet I prefer the simple plan, and I believe that all these devices are contrary to true wisdom.

There is a disposition in some quarters to insist that any concessions to France by Great Britain and the United States, affecting reparation and inter-Ally debt, should be conditional on France's acceptance of a more pacific policy towards the rest of the world than that to which she herself appears to be inclined. I hope that France will abandon her opposition to proposals for reduced military and naval establishments. What a handicap her youth will suffer if she maintains conscription whilst her neighbours, voluntarily or involuntarily, have abandoned it! Does she realise the impossibility of friendship between Great Britain and *any* neighbouring power which embarks on a large programme of submarines? I hope, too, that France will forget her dangerous ambitions in Central Europe and will limit strictly those in the Near East; for both are based on rubbishy foundations and will bring her no good. That she has anything to fear from Germany in the future which we can foresee, except what she may herself provoke, is a delusion. When Germany has recovered her strength and pride, as in due time she will, many years must pass before she again casts her eyes westward. Germany's future now lies to the east, and in that direction her hopes and ambitions, when they revive, will certainly turn.

France has an opportunity now of consolidating her national

position into one of the stablest, safest, richest on the face of the earth; self-contained; well- but not over-populated; the heir of a peculiar and splendid civilisation. Neither whining about devastated districts, which are easily repaired, nor boasting of military hegemonies, which can quickly ruin her, let her lift up her head as the leader and mistress of Europe in the peaceful practices of the mind.

Nevertheless, these objects are not to be gained by bargaining and cannot be imposed from without. Therefore they must not be dragged into the reparation settlement. This settlement must be offered France on one condition only—that she accepts it. But if, like Shylock, she claims her pound of flesh, then let the law prevail. Let her have her bond, and let us have our bonds too. Let her get what she can from Germany and pay what she owes to the United States and England.

The chief question for dispute is, perhaps, whether an annual payment by Germany of £63 million (gold) is enough. I admit that the payment of a somewhat larger sum may prove to be within her capacity. But I recommend this figure because on the one hand it is sufficient to restore the destruction done in France, yet on the other is not so crushing that, to make Germany pay it, we need be in a position to invade her every spring and autumn. We must fix the payment at an amount which Germany herself will recognise as not unjust, and which is sufficiently within her maximum capacity to leave her some incentive to work and pay it off.

Suppose that we knew the theoretical maximum of Germany's capacity to produce and sell abroad a surplus of goods, or could hit on some sliding scale which would automatically absorb year by year whatever surplus there was; should we be wise to demand it? The project of extracting at the point of the bayonet—for that is what it would mean—a payment so heavy that it would never be paid voluntarily, and to go on doing this until all the makers of the Peace Treaty of Versailles have been long dead and buried in their local Valhallas, is neither good nor sensible.

My own proposals, moderate though they may seem in comparison with others, throw on Germany a very great burden. They procure for France an enormous benefit. Frenchmen, having fed to satiety on imaginary figures, are nearly ready, I think, to find a surprising flavour and piquancy in real ones. Let them consider what a tremendous financial strength my scheme would give them. Freed from external debt, they would receive in real values each year for thirty years a payment equivalent in gold to nearly half the gold reserve now held by the Bank of France; and at the end of the set period Germany would have paid back ten times what she took after 1870.

Is it for Englishmen to complain? Are they really losers? One cannot cast up a balance sheet between incommensurables. But peace and amity might be won for Europe. And England is only asked (as I fancy she knows pretty well, by now, in her bones) to give up something which she will never get anyhow. The alternative is that we and the United States will be jockeyed out of our claims amidst a general international disgust.

# APPENDIX OF DOCUMENTS

## I. THE SPA AGREEMENT, JULY 1920

(*A*) *Summary*[1] *of the agreement upon reparations between the allies,
signed by the British Empire, France, Italy, Japan, Belgium, and Portugal*

Article 1 provides that in pursuance of the Treaty of Versailles the sums received from Germany for reparations shall be divided in the following proportions:

| | |
|---|---|
| France | 52 per cent |
| British Empire | 22 per cent |
| Italy | 10 per cent |
| Belgium | 8 per cent |
| Japan and Portugal | ¾ of 1 per cent each |

The remaining 6½ per cent is reserved for the Serbo-Croat–Slovene State and for Greece, Roumania, and other Powers not signatories of the Agreement.

Article 2 provides that the aggregate amount received for reparation from Austria-Hungary and Bulgaria, together with amounts that may be received in respect of the liberation of territories belonging to the former Austro-Hungarian monarchy, shall be divided:

(*a*) As to half in the proportions mentioned in Article 1.

(*b*) As to the other half, Italy shall receive 40 per cent, while 60 per cent is reserved for Greece, Roumania, and the Serbo-Croat–Slovene State and other Powers entitled to reparations but not signatories of the Agreement.

Article 3 provides that the Allied governments shall adopt measures to facilitate if necessary the issue by Germany of loans destined for the internal requirements of that country and to the prompt discharge of the German debt to the Allies.

Article 4 deals in detail with the keeping of accounts by the Reparation Commission.

Article 5 secures to Belgium her priority of £100 million gold and enumerates the securities affected by such priority.[2]

---

[1] The following is the official summary issued at the time. The complete text of the Agreement has not been published.

[2] Of which the most tangible were 100 million Danish kroner payable in respect of Schleswig, certain sums were from Luxembourg for coal, any balance available in respect of German ships seized as prizes in Brazilian ports, and any balance available towards reparation out of German assets in the United States.

Article 6 deals with the valuation of ships surrendered under the various Peace Treaties, and provides for the allocation of sums received for the hire of such ships. It deals also with questions outstanding as to the decisions taken by the Belgian Prize Courts. Belgium receives compensation out of the shares of the other Allied Powers.

Article 7 refers to the Allied cruisers, floating docks, and material handed over under the Protocol of 10 January 1920, as compensation for the German warships which were sunk.

Article 8 declares that the same Protocol shall apply to the proceeds of the sale of ships and war material surrendered under the naval clauses of the Treaty, virtually including the proceeds of naval war material sold by the Reparation Commission.

Article 9 gives Italy an absolutely prior claim to certain specified sums as a set-off to amounts due to her by Austria-Hungary and Bulgaria.

Article 10 reserves the rights of Poland and declares that this Agreement shall not apply to her.

Article 11 maintains the rights of countries who lent money to Belgium before 11 November 1918, and makes provision for repayment immediately after satisfaction of the Belgian claim to priority in respect of £100 million.

Article 12 maintains the rights of the Allied Powers to the repayments of credits granted to ex-enemy powers for the purposes of relief.

Article 13 reserves the question of fixing the cost of the armies of occupation in Germany on a uniform basis for discussion with the United States of America.

### (B) *The Allied note to Germany on the subject of coal deliveries*

1. The German government undertakes to place at the disposal of the Allies, from 1 August 1920 for the ensuing six months, 2 million tons of coal per month, this figure having been approved by the Reparation Commission.

2. The Allied governments will credit the reparation accounts with the value of this coal, as far as it is delivered by rail or inland navigation, and it will be valued at the German internal price in accordance with Paragraph 6 (A), Annex V, Part VIII, of the Treaty of Versailles. In addition, in consideration of the admission of the right of the Allies to have coal of specified kind and quality delivered to them, a premium of five gold marks, payable in cash by the party taking delivery, shall be applied to the acquisition of foodstuffs for the German miners.

3. During the period of the coal deliveries provided for above, the stipulations of Paragraphs 2, 3, and 4 of the draft Control Protocol of 11 July 1920

shall be put in force at once in the modified form of the Annex hereto. (See below.)

4. An agreement shall be made forthwith between the Allies for distribution of the Upper Silesian coal output by a Commission on which Germany will be represented. This agreement shall be submitted for the approval of the Reparation Commission.

5. The Commission, on which the Germans shall be represented, shall meet forthwith at Essen. Its purpose shall be to seek means by which the conditions of life among the miners with regard to food and clothing can be improved, with a view to the better working of the mines.

6. The Allied governments declare their readiness to make advances to Germany equal in amount to the difference between the price paid under Paragraph 2 above, and the export price of German coal, f.o.b. in German ports, or the English export price, f.o.b. in English ports, whichever may be the lowest, as laid down in Paragraph 6 (B) of Annex V, Part VIII, of the Treaty of Versailles. These advances shall be made in accordance with Articles 235 and 251 of the Treaty of Versailles. They shall enjoy an absolute priority over all other allied claims on Germany. The advances shall be made at the end of each month, in accordance with the number of tons delivered and the average f.o.b. price of coal during the period. Advances on account shall be made by the Allies at the end of the first month, without waiting for exact figures.

7. If by 15 November 1920 it is ascertained that the total deliveries for August, September, and October 1920 have not reached 6 million tons, the Allies will proceed to the occupation of a further portion of German territory, either the region of the Ruhr or some other.

### Annex

1. A permanent delegation of the Reparation Commission will be set up at Berlin, whose mission will be to satisfy itself by the following means that the deliveries of coal to the Allies provided for under the Agreement of 15 July 1920 shall be carried out: The programmes for the general distribution of output, with details of origin and kind, on the one hand, and the orders given to ensure deliveries to the Allied Powers on the other hand, shall be drawn up by the responsible German authorities and submitted by them for the approval of the said delegation a reasonable time before their despatch to the executive bodies responsible for their execution.

2. No modification in the said programme which may involve a reduction in the amount of the deliveries to the Allies shall be put into effect without prior approval of the Delegation of the Reparation Commission in Berlin.

3. The Reparation Commission, to which the German government must

periodically report the execution by the competent bodies of the orders for deliveries to the Allies, will notify to the interested powers any infraction of the principles adopted herein.

## 2. THE PARIS DECISIONS,[1] 29 JANUARY 1921

1. In satisfaction of the obligations laid on her by Articles 231 and 232 of the Treaty of Versailles, Germany shall pay, apart from the restitutions which she must effect in conformity with Article 238 and all obligations under the Treaty:

(1) Fixed annuities, payable in equal instalments at the end of each six months, as follows:

(*a*) Two annuities of 2 milliard gold marks (1 May 1921–1 May 1923).
(*b*) Three annuities of 3 milliard gold marks (1 May 1923–1 May 1926).
(*c*) Three annuities of 4 milliard gold marks (1 May 1926–1 May 1929).
(*d*) Three annuities of 5 milliard gold marks (1 May 1929–1 May 1932).
(*e*) Thirty-one annuities of 6 milliard gold marks (1 May 1932–1 May 1963).

(2) Forty-two annuities, reckoning from 1 May 1921, equivalent to 12 per cent of the value of Germany's exports, levied on the receipts from them and payable in gold two months after the conclusion of each six-monthly period.

To ensure that (2) above shall be completely carried out, Germany will accord to the Reparation Commission every facility for verifying the amount of the exports and for establishing the necessary supervision.

2. The German government shall deliver forthwith to the Reparation Commission bearer bonds payable at the due dates laid down in Article 1 (1) of the present scheme, and of an amount equal to each of the six-monthly instalments payable thereunder. Instructions will be given with the object of facilitating, on the part of such powers as may require it, the mobilisation of the portion accruing to them under the agreements which they have established amongst themselves.

3. Germany shall be entitled at any time to anticipate the fixed portion of her obligation.

Payments made by her in anticipation shall be applied in reduction of the fixed annuities prescribed in Article 1 (1), discounted at a rate of 8 per cent up to 1 May 1923, 6 per cent from 1 May 1923 to 1 May 1925, and 5 per cent after 1 May 1925.

4. Germany shall not embark on any credit operation abroad, directly or indirectly, without the approval of the Reparation Commission. This

---

[1] So far as I am aware, no complete official text of these decisions has been published in English. The above is translated from the French text.

restriction applies to the government of the German Empire, the government of the German States, German provincial and municipal authorities, and also to companies and enterprises controlled by these governments and authorities.

5. In pursuance of Article 248 of the Treaty of Versailles all the assets and revenues of the German Empire and its constituent States are held in guarantee of the complete execution by Germany of the provisions of this scheme.

The receipts of the German customs, by land and sea, in particular the receipts of all import and export duties and all supplementary taxes, constitute a special pledge for the execution of the present Agreement.

No modification shall be introduced, liable to diminish the yield of the customs, without the Reparation Commission approving the customs legislation and regulations of Germany.

The whole of the receipts of the German customs shall be credited to the account of the German government, by a Receiver-General of the German customs, nominated by the German government with the assent of the Reparation Commission.

In the event of Germany failing to meet one of the payments laid down in the present scheme:

(1) The whole or part of the receipts of the German customs shall be taken over from the Receiver-General of the German customs by the Reparation Commission and applied by it to the obligations in which Germany has defaulted. In this event the Reparation Commission shall, if it deems necessary, itself assume the administration and collection of the customs receipts.

(2) The Reparation Commission shall be entitled, in addition, to require the German government to impose such higher tariffs or to take such other measures to increase its resources as it may deem indispensable.

(3) If this injunction is without effect, the Commission shall be entitled to declare the German government in default and to notify this state of affairs to the governments of the Allied and Associated Powers who shall take such measures as they think justified.

(Signed)  HENRI JASPAR
D. LLOYD GEORGE
ARISTIDE BRIAND
C. SFORZA
K. ISHII

*Paris, 29 January 1921*

### 3. CLAIMS SUBMITTED TO THE REPARATION COMMISSION BY THE VARIOUS ALLIED NATIONS, AS PUBLISHED BY THE COMMISSION,[1] 23 FEBRUARY 1921

#### FRANCE

#### I. *Damage to property (reconstitution values)*

|  | Frs. (paper) |
|---|---|
| Industrial damages | 38,882,521,479 |
| Damage to buildings (*propriété bâtie*) | 36,892,500,000 |
| Damage to furniture and fittings (*dommages mobiliers*) | 25,119,500,000 |
| Damage to land (*propriété non bâtie*) | 21,671,546,225 |
| Damage to State property | 1,958,217,193 |
| Damage to public works | 2,583,299,425 |
| Other damages | 2,359,865,000 |
| Shipping losses | 5,009,618,722 |
| Damages suffered in Algeria and colonies | 10,710,000 |
| Damages suffered abroad | 2,094,825,000 |
| Interest at 5 per cent on the principal (33,000 million francs, in round figures, between 11 November 1918 and 1 May 1921, or 30 months), say, in round figures | 4,125,000,000 |

#### II. *Injuries to persons*

|  | Frs. (paper) |
|---|---|
| Military pensions | 60,045,696,000 |
| Allowances to families of mobilised men | 12,936,956,824 |
| Pensions accorded to civilian victims of the war and their dependants | 514,465,000 |
| Ill-treatment inflicted on civilians and prisoners of war | 1,869,230,000 |
| Assistance given to prisoners of war | 976,906,000 |
| Insufficiency of salaries and wages | 223,123,313 |
| Exactions by Germany to the detriment of the civilian population | 1,267,615,939 |
| Total of the French claims | 218,541,596,120 |

#### GREAT BRITAIN

|  | £ | Frs. |
|---|---|---|
| Damage to property | 7,936,456 | |
| Shipping losses | 763,000,000 | |
| Losses abroad | 24,940,559 | |
| Damage to river and canal shipping | 4,000,000 | |
| Military pensions | 1,706,800,000 | |
| Allowances to families of mobilised men | | 7,597,832,086 |
| Pensions for civilian victims | 35,915,579 | |
| Ill-treatment inflicted on civilians and prisoners | 95,746 | |
| Assistance to prisoners of war | 12,663 | |
| Insufficiency of salaries and wages | 6,372 | |
|  | £2,542,707,375 | Frs. 7,597,832,086 |

[1] The Commission published at the same time a warning that it had not adopted these claims, but was about to examine them.

### ITALY

| | |
|---|---|
| Damage to property | Lire 20,933,547,500 |
| Shipping losses | £128,000,000 |
| Military pensions | Francs 31,041,000,000 |
| Allowances to families of mobilised men | Francs 6,885,130,395 |
| Civilian victims of the war and prisoners | Lire 12,153,289,000 |
| Total | Lire 33,086,836,000 |
| Total | Francs 37,926,130,395 |
| Total | £128,000,000 |

### BELGIUM

| | |
|---|---|
| Damage to property (present value) | Belgian Frs. 29,773,939,099 |
| Shipping losses (present value) | Belgian Frs. 180,708,250 |
| Military pensions | French Frs. 1,637,285,512 |
| Allowances to families of mobilised men | French Frs. 737,930,484 |
| Civilian victims and prisoners of war | Belgian Frs. 4,295,998,454 |
| Total | Belgian Frs. 34,254,645,893 |
| Total | French Frs. 2,375,215,996 |

The other claims may be summarised as follows:

| | |
|---|---|
| Japan | 297,593,000 yen (shipping losses). |
| | 454,063,000 yen (allowances to families of mobilised men). |
| | 832,774,000 yen. |
| Jugoslavia | 8,496,091,000 dinars (damage to property). |
| | 19,219,700,112 francs (injuries to persons). |
| Roumania | 9,734,015,287 gold francs (property losses). |
| | 9,296,663,076 gold francs (military pensions). |
| | 11,652,009,978 gold francs (civilians and prisoners of war). |
| | 31,099,400,188 gold francs. |
| Portugal | 1,944,261 contos (1,574,907 contos for property loss). |
| Greece | 4,992,788,739 gold francs (1,883,181,542 francs for property loss). |
| Brazil | £1,216,714 (shipping £1,189,144), plus 598,405 francs. |
| Czechoslovakia | 6,944,228,296 francs and 5,614,947,990 kroner (war losses). |
| | 618,204,007 francs and 1,448,169,845 kroner (Bolshevist invasion). |
| | 7,612,432,103 francs and 7,063,117,135 kroner. |
| Siam | 9,179,298 marks, gold, plus 1,169,821 francs. |
| Bolivia | £16,000. |
| Peru | £56,236, plus 107,389 francs. |
| Haiti | $80,000, plus 532,593 francs. |
| Cuba | $801,135. |
| Liberia | $3,977,135. |
| Poland | 21,913,269,740 francs gold, plus 500,000,000 marks gold. |

European Danube Commission: 1,834,800 francs gold, 15,048 francs French, and 488,051 lei.

## 4. THE FIRST ULTIMATUM OF LONDON, 3 MARCH 1921

The following declaration was delivered to Dr Simons by Mr Lloyd George, speaking on behalf of the British and allied governments, by word of mouth:

'The Allies have been conferring upon the whole position and I am now authorised to make this declaration on their behalf:

"The Treaty of Versailles was signed less than two years ago. The German Government have already defaulted in respect of some of its most important provisions: the delivery for trial of the criminals, who have offended against the laws of war, disarmament, the payment in cash or in kind of 20,000 million of gold marks (£1,000 million). These are some of the provisions. The Allies have displayed no harsh insistence upon the letter of their bond. They have extended time, they have even modified the character of their demands; but each time the German Government failed them.

"In spite of the Treaty and of the honourable undertaking given at Spa, the criminals have not yet been tried, let alone punished, although the evidence has been in the hands of the German Government for months. Military organisations, some of them open, some clandestine, have been allowed to spring up all over the country, equipped with arms that ought to have been surrendered. If the German Government had shown in respect of reparations a sincere desire to help the allies to repair the terrible losses inflicted upon them by the act of aggression of which the German Imperialist Government was guilty, we should still have been ready as before to make all allowances for the legitimate difficulties of Germany. But the proposals put forward have reluctantly convinced the Allies either that the German Government does not intend to carry out its Treaty obligations, or that it has not the strength to insist, in the face of selfish and short-sighted opposition, upon the necessary sacrifices being made.

"If that is due to the fact that German opinion will not permit it, that makes the situation still more serious, and renders it all the more necessary that the allies should bring the leaders of public opinion once more face to face with facts. The first essential fact for them to realise is this—that the Allies, whilst prepared to listen to every reasonable plea arising out of Germany's difficulties, cannot allow any further paltering with the Treaty.

### The Ultimatum

"We have therefore decided—having regard to the infractions already committed, to the determination indicated in these proposals that Germany means still further to defy and explain away the Treaty, and to the challenge issued not merely in these proposals but in official statements made in Germany by the German Government—that we must act upon the assumption that the German Government are not merely in default, but deliberately in default; and unless we hear by Monday that Germany is either prepared to accept the Paris decisions or to submit proposals which will in other ways be an equally satisfactory discharge of her obligations under the Treaty of Versailles (subject to the concessions made in the Paris proposals), we shall, as from that date, take the following course under the Treaty of Versailles.

"The Allies are agreed:

(1) To occupy the towns of Duisburg, Ruhrort, and Düsseldorf, on the right bank of the Rhine.

(2) To obtain powers from their respective Parliaments requiring their nationals to pay a certain proportion of all payments due to Germany on German goods to their several Governments, such proportion to be retained on account of reparations. (This is in respect of goods purchased either in this country or in any other Allied country from Germany.)

(3) (a) The amount of the duties collected by the German Customs houses on the external frontiers of the occupied territories to be paid to the Reparation Commission.

(b) These duties to continue to be levied in accordance with the German tariff.

(c) A line of Customs houses to be temporarily established on the Rhine and at the boundary of the *têtes des ponts* occupied by the Allied troops; the tariff to be levied on this line, both on the entry and export of goods, to be determined by the Allied High Commission of the Rhine territory in conformity with the instructions of the Allied Governments."'

## 5. THE GERMAN COUNTER-PROPOSAL, AS TRANSMITTED TO THE UNITED STATES GOVERNMENT, 24 APRIL 1921

The United States Government have, by their Note of 22 April, opened the possibility, in a way which is thankfully acknowledged, of solving the reparations problem once more by negotiations ere a solution is effected by coercive measures. The German Government appreciates this step in its full importance. They have in the following proposals endeavoured to offer that which according to their convictions represents the utmost limit which Germany's economic resources can bear, even with the most favourable developments:

1. Germany expresses her readiness to acknowledge for reparation purposes a total liability of 50 milliard gold marks (present value). Germany is also prepared to pay the equivalent of this sum in annuities, adapted to her

economic capacity up to an aggregate of 200 milliard gold marks. Germany proposes to mobilise her liability in the following way:

2. Germany to raise at once an international loan, of which amount, rate of interest, and amortisation quota are to be agreed on. Germany will participate in this loan, and its terms, in order to secure the greatest possible success, will contain special concessions, and generally be made as favourable as possible. Proceeds of this loan to be placed at the disposal of the Allies.

3. On the amount of her liability not covered by the international loan Germany is prepared to pay interest and amortisation quota in accordance with her economic capacity. In present circumstances she considers the rate of 4 per cent the highest possible.

4. Germany is prepared to let the Powers concerned have the benefit of improvements in her economic and financial situation. For this purpose the amortisation quota should be made variable. In case an improvement should take place, the quota would rise, whilst it would correspondingly fall if developments should be in the other direction. To regulate such variations an index scheme would have to be prepared.

5. To accelerate the redemption of the balance, Germany is ready to assist with all her resources in the reconstruction of the devastated territories. She considers reconstruction the most pressing part of reparation, because it is the most effective way to combat the hatred and misery caused by the war. She is prepared to undertake, herself, the rebuilding of townships, villages, and hamlets, or to assist in the reconstruction with labour, material, and her other resources, in any way the Allies may desire. The cost of such labour and material she would pay herself. (Full details about this matter have been communicated to the Reparation Commission.)

6. Apart from any reconstruction work Germany is prepared to supply for the same purpose, to States concerned, any other materials, and to render them any other services as far as possible on a purely commercial basis.

7. To prove the sincerity of her intention to make reparation at once, and in an unmistakable way, Germany is prepared to place immediately at the disposal of the Reparation Commission the amount of one milliard gold marks in the following manner: First, 150 million gold marks in gold, silver, and foreign bills; secondly, 850 million gold marks in Treasury bills, to be redeemed within a period not exceeding three months by foreign bills and other foreign values.

8. Germany is further prepared, if the United States and the Allies should so desire, to assume part of the indebtedness of the Allies to the United States as far as her economic capacity will allow her.

9. In respect of the method by which the German expenditures for reparations purposes should be credited against her total liability, Germany

proposes that prices and values should be fixed by a commission of experts.

10. Germany is prepared to secure subscribers for the loan in every possible way by assigning to them public properties or public income in a way to be arranged for.

11. By the acceptance of these proposals all other German liabilities on reparation account are cancelled, and German private property abroad released.

12. Germany considers that her proposals can only be realised if the system of sanctions is done away with at once; if the present basis of German production is not further diminished; and if the German nation is again admitted to the world's commerce and freed of all unproductive expenditure.

These proposals testify to the German firm will to make good damage caused by the war up to the limit of her economic capacity. The amounts offered, as well as mode of payment, depend on this capacity. As far as differences of opinion as to this capacity exist, the German Government recommend that they be examined by a commission of recognised experts acceptable to all the interested Governments. She declares herself ready in advance to accept as binding any decision come to by it. Should the United States Government consider negotiations could be facilitated by giving the proposals another form, the German Government would be thankful if their attention were drawn to points in which the United States Government consider an alteration desirable. The German Government would also readily receive any other proposals the United States Government might feel inclined to make.

The German Government is too firmly convinced that the peace and welfare of the world depend on a prompt, just, and fair solution of the reparation problem not to do everything in their power to put the United States in a position which enables them to bring the matter to the attention of the Allied Governments.

*Berlin*, 24 *April* 1921

6. THE ASSESSMENT ANNOUNCED BY THE REPARATION
COMMISSION, 30 APRIL 1921

The Reparation Commission, in discharge of the provisions of Article 233 of the Treaty of Versailles, has reached a unanimous decision to fix at 132 milliard gold marks the total of the damages for which reparation is due by Germany under Article 232 (2) and Part VIII, Annex I of the said Treaty.

In fixing this figure the Commission have made the necessary deductions from the total of damages to cover restitutions effected or to be effected in discharge of Article 238, so that no credit will be due to Germany from the fact of these restitutions.

The Commission have not included in the above figure the sum corresponding to the obligation, which falls on Germany as an addition in virtue of Article 232 (3), 'to make reimbursement of all sums which Belgium has borrowed from the Allied and Associated Governments up to 11 November 1918, together with interest at the rate of 5 per cent per annum on such sums'.

## 7. THE SECOND ULTIMATUM OF LONDON, 5 MAY 1921

The Allied Powers, taking note of the fact that, in spite of the successive concessions made by the Allies since the signature of the Treaty of Versailles, and in spite of the warnings and sanctions agreed upon at Spa and at Paris, as well as of the sanctions announced in London and since applied, the German Government is still in default in the fulfilment of the obligations incumbent upon it under the terms of the Treaty of Versailles as regards (1) disarmament; (2) the payment due on 1 May 1921, under Article 235 of the Treaty, which the Reparation Commission has already called upon it to make at this date; (3) the trial of the war criminals as further provided for by the Allied Notes of 13 February and 7 May 1920; and (4) certain other important respects, notably those which arise under Articles 264 to 267, 269, 273, 321, 322, and 327 of the Treaty, decide:

(*a*) To proceed forthwith with such preliminary measures as may be required for the occupation of the Ruhr Valley by the Allied Forces on the Rhine in the contingency provided for in Paragraph (*d*) of this Note.

(*b*) In accordance with Article 233 of the Treaty to invite the Reparation Commission to prescribe to the German Government without delay the time and manner for securing and discharging the entire obligation incumbent upon that Government, and to announce their decision on this point to the German Government at latest on 6 May.

(*c*) To call upon the German Government categorically to declare within a period of six days from the receipt of the above decision its resolve (1) to carry out without reserve or condition their obligations as defined by the Reparation Commission; (2) to accept without reserve or condition the guarantees in respect of those obligations prescribed by the Reparation Commission; (3) to carry out without reserve or delay the measures of military, naval, and aerial disarmament notified to the German Government by the Allied Powers in their Note of 29 January 1921, those overdue being completed at once, and the remainder by the prescribed dates; (4) to carry out without reserve or delay the trial of the war criminals and the other unfulfilled portions of the Treaty referred to in the first paragraph of this Note.

(*d*) Failing fulfilment by the German Government of the above conditions by 12 May, to proceed to the occupation of the Valley of the Ruhr and to take all other military and naval measures that may be required. Such occupation will continue so long as Germany fails to comply with the conditions summarised in Paragraph (*c*).

(Signed)   HENRI JASPAR

A. BRIAND

D. LLOYD GEORGE

C. SFORZA

HAYASHI

*Schedule of payments prescribing the time and manner for securing and discharging the entire obligation of Germany for reparation under Articles 231, 232, and 233 of the Treaty of Versailles*

The Reparation Commission has, in accordance with Article 233 of the Treaty of Versailles, fixed the time and manner for securing and discharging the entire obligation of Germany for Reparation under Articles 231, 232, and 233 of the Treaty as follows:

This determination is without prejudice to the duty of Germany to make restitution under Article 238, or to other obligations under the Treaty.

1. Germany will perform in the manner laid down in this schedule her obligations to pay the total fixed in accordance with Articles 231, 232, and 233 of the Treaty of Versailles by the Commission—viz. 132 milliards of gold marks (£6,600 million) less (*a*) the amount already paid on account of reparation; (*b*) sums which may from time to time be credited to Germany in respect of State properties in ceded territory, etc.; and (*c*) any sums received from other enemy or ex-enemy Powers in respect of which the Commission may decide that credits should be given to Germany, *plus* the amount of the Belgian debt to the Allies, the amounts of these deductions and additions to be determined later by the Commission.

2. Germany shall create and deliver to the Commission in substitution for bonds already delivered or deliverable under Paragraph 12 (*c*) of Annex 2 of Part VIII (Reparation) of the Treaty of Versailles the bonds hereinafter described.

(*A*) Bonds for an amount of 12 milliard gold marks (£600 million). These bonds shall be created and delivered at latest on 1 July 1921. There shall be an annual payment from funds to be provided by Germany as prescribed in this agreement, in each year from 1 May 1921, equal in amount to 6 per cent of the nominal value of the issued bonds, out of which there shall be paid interest at 5 per cent per annum, payable half-yearly on the bonds outstanding at any time, and the balance to sinking fund for the redemption of the bonds by annual drawings at par. These bonds are hereinafter referred to as bonds of Series (*A*).

(*B*) Bonds for a further amount of 38 milliard gold marks (£1,900 million). These bonds shall be created and delivered at the latest on 1 November 1921. There shall be an annual payment from funds to be provided by Germany as prescribed in this agreement in each year from 1 November 1921, equal in amount to 6 per cent of the nominal value of the issued bonds, out of which there shall be paid interest at 5 per cent per annum, payable half-yearly on the bonds outstanding at any time and the balance to sinking fund for the redemption of the bonds by annual drawings at par. These bonds are hereinafter referred to as bonds of Series (*B*).

(*C*) Bonds for 82 milliards of gold marks (£4,100 million), subject to such subsequent adjustment by creation or cancellation of bonds as may be required under Paragraph (1). These bonds shall be created and delivered to the Reparation Commission, without coupons attached, at latest on 1 November 1921; they shall be issued by the Commission as and when it is satisfied that the payments which Germany undertakes to make in pursuance of this agreement are sufficient to provide for the payment of interest and sinking fund on such bonds. There shall be an annual payment from funds to be provided by Germany as prescribed in this agreement in each year from the date of issue by the Reparation Commission equal in amount to 6 per cent of the nominal value of the issued bonds, out of which shall be paid interest at 5 per cent per annum, payable half-yearly on the bonds outstanding at any time, and the balance to sinking fund for the redemption of the bonds by annual drawings at par. The German Government shall supply to the Commission coupons for such bonds as and when issued by the Commission. These bonds are hereinafter referred to as bonds of Series (*C*).

3. The bonds provided for in Article 2 shall be signed German Government bearer bonds, in such form and in such denominations as the Reparation Commission shall prescribe for the purpose of making them marketable, and shall be free of all German taxes and charges of every description present or future.

Subject to the provisions of Articles 248 and 251 of the Treaty of Versailles these bonds shall be secured on the whole of the assets and revenues of the German Empire and the German States, and in particular on the specific assets and revenues specified in Article 7 of the agreement. The service of the bonds of Series (*A*), (*B*), and (*C*) shall be a first, second, and third charge respectively on the said assets and revenues and shall be met by the payments to be made by Germany under this Schedule.

4. Germany shall pay in each year until the redemption of the bonds provided for in Article 2 by means of the sinking funds attached thereto:

(1) A sum of two milliard gold marks (£100 million).

(2) (*a*) A sum equivalent to 25 per cent of the value of her exports in each period of 12 months starting from 1 May 1921, as determined by the Commission; or

(*b*) Alternatively an equivalent amount as fixed in accordance with any other index proposed by Germany and accepted by the Commission.

(3) A further sum equivalent to 1 per cent of the value of her exports as above defined, or alternatively an equivalent amount fixed as provided in (*b*) above.

Provided always that when Germany shall have discharged all her obligations under this Schedule, other than her liability in respect of outstanding bonds, the amount to be paid in each year under this paragraph shall be reduced to the amount required in that year to meet the interest and sinking fund on the bonds then outstanding.

Subject to the provisions of Article 5, the payments to be made in respect of Paragraph (1) above shall be made quarterly before the end of each quarter, i.e. before 15 January, 15 April, 15 July, and 15 October each year, and the payments in respect of Paragraphs (2) and (3) above shall be made quarterly, 15 November, 15 February, 15 May, 15 August, and calculated on the basis of the exports in the last quarter but one preceding that quarter, the first payment to be made 15 November 1921.

5. Germany will pay within 25 days from this notification one milliard gold marks (£50 million) in gold or approved foreign bills or in drafts at three months on the German Treasury, endorsed by approved German banks and payable in London, Paris, New York, or any other place designated by the Reparation Commission. These payments will be treated as the first two quarterly instalments of the payments provided for in compliance with Article 4 (1).

6. The Commission will within 25 days from this notification, in accordance with Paragraph 12 (*d*), Annex II of the Treaty as amended, establish the special Sub-Commission to be called the Committee of Guarantees. The Committee of Guarantees will consist of representatives of the Allied Powers now represented on the Reparation Commission, including a representative of the United States of America, in the event of that Government desiring to make the appointment.

The Committee shall co-opt not more than three representatives of nationals of other Powers whenever it shall appear to the Commission that a sufficient portion of the bonds to be issued under this agreement is held by nationals of such Powers to justify their representation on the Committee of Guarantees.

7. The Committee of Guarantees is charged with the duty of securing the application of Articles 241 and 248 of the Treaty of Versailles.

It shall supervise the application to the service of the bonds provided for in Article 2 of the funds assigned as security for the payments to be made by Germany under Paragraph 4. The funds to be so assigned shall be:

(*a*) The proceeds of all German maritime and land Customs and duties, and in particular the proceeds of all import and export duties.

(*b*) The proceeds of the levy of 25 per cent on the value of all exports from Germany, except those exports upon which a levy of not less than 25 per cent is applied under the legislation referred to in Article 9.

(*c*) The proceeds of such direct or indirect taxes or any other funds as may be proposed by the German Government and accepted by the Committee of Guarantees in addition to or in substitution for the funds specified in (*a*) or (*b*) above.

The assigned funds shall be paid to accounts to be opened in the name of the Committee and supervised by it, in gold or in foreign currency approved by the Committee. The equivalent of the 25 per cent levy referred to in Paragraph (*b*) shall be paid in German currency by the German Government to the exporter.

The German Government shall notify to the Committee of Guarantees any proposed action which may tend to diminish the proceeds of any of the assigned funds, and shall, if the Committee demand it, substitute some other approved funds.

The Committee of Guarantees shall be charged further with the duty of conducting on behalf of the Commission the examination provided for in Paragraph 12 (*b*) of Annex 2 to Part VIII of the Treaty of Versailles, and of verifying on behalf of the said Commission, and if necessary of correcting, the amount declared by the German Government as the value of German exports for the purpose of the calculation of the sum payable in each year under Article 4 (2) and the amounts of the funds assigned under this Article to the service of the bonds. The Committee shall be entitled to take such measures as it may deem necessary for the proper discharge of its duties.

The Committee of Guarantees is not authorised to interfere in German administration.

8. Germany shall on demand, subject to the prior approval of the Com-

mission, provide such material and labour as any of the Allied Powers may require towards the restoration of the devastated areas of that Power, or to enable any Allied Power to proceed with the restoration or development of its industrial or economic life. The value of such material and labour shall be determined by a valuer appointed by Germany and a valuer appointed by the Power concerned and, in default of agreement, by a referee nominated by the Commission. This provision as to valuation does not apply to deliveries under Annexes III, IV, V, and VI to Part VIII of the Treaty.

9. Germany shall take every necessary measure of legislative and administrative action to facilitate the operation of the German Reparation (Recovery) Act, 1921, in force in the United Kingdom, and of any similar legislation enacted by any Allied Power, so long as such legislation remains in force. Payments effected by the operation of such legislation shall be credited to Germany on account of the payment to be made by her under Article 4 (2). The equivalent in German currency shall be paid by the German Government to the exporter.

10. Payment for all services rendered, all deliveries in kind, and all receipts under Article 9 shall be made to the Reparation Commission by the Allied Power receiving the same in cash or current coupons within one month of the receipt thereof, and shall be credited to Germany on account of the payments to be made by her under Article 4.

11. The sum payable under Article 4 (3) and the surplus receipts by the Commission under Article 4 (1) and (2) in each year, not required for the payment of interest and sinking fund on bonds outstanding in that year, shall be accumulated and applied so far as they will extend, at such times as the Commission may think fit, by the Commission in paying simple interest not exceeding $2\frac{1}{2}$ per cent per annum from 1 May 1921 to 1 May 1926, and thereafter at a rate not exceeding 5 per cent on the balance of the debt not covered by the bonds then issued. No interest thereon shall be payable otherwise.

12. The present Schedule does not modify the provisions securing the execution of the Treaty of Versailles, which are applicable to the stipulations of the present Schedule.

## 8. THE WIESBADEN AGREEMENT, 6 OCTOBER 1921

This Agreement, signed by M. Loucheur and Herr Rathenau at Wiesbaden on 6 October 1921 is a lengthy document, consisting of a protocol, memorandum and annex. The effective clauses are to be found mainly in the annex. The full text has been published in a British White Paper [Cmd. 1547]. This White Paper also contains (1) an explanatory memorandum, (2) the decision of the Reparation Commission, and (3) a report from Sir John Bradbury to the British Treasury. Extracts from these three documents are given below.

### 1. *Explanatory memorandum*

In order to understand the arrangements proposed by the Wiesbaden Agreement, it is necessary to bear in mind certain provisions of the Treaty of Versailles, the application of which is affected by it.

The Treaty itself provides in the Reparation Chapter, Part VIII, and in some of its Annexes, for the partial liquidation of Germany's reparation indebtedness by deliveries in kind. The important passages in this connection are Paragraph 19 of Annex II and Annex IV, which together make extensive provision for the delivery, through the Reparation Commission, to the Allied and Associated Powers of machinery, equipment, tools, reconstruction material and, in general, all such material and labour as is necessary to enable any Allied Power to proceed with the restoration or development of its industrial or economic life.

Germany's obligation being stated in terms of gold and not in terms of commodities, provision has necessarily been made in all cases for crediting Germany, from time to time, with the fair value, as assessed by the Reparation Commission, of such deliveries. Moreover, since the proportions received by the respective Powers in kind need not necessarily correspond exactly with their respective shares in Germany's reparation payments, as determined by Inter-Allied agreement, provision is further necessarily made in the Treaty to render each Power accountable not only to Germany, but to the Reparation Commission, for the value of these deliveries. Thus, on the one hand, the Treaty stipulates as between the Allies and Germany that the value of services under the Annexes shall be credited towards the liquidation of Germany's general obligation, and the Schedule of Payments assigns the value of Annex deliveries to the service of the bonds handed over by Germany as security for her debt. On the other hand, the Treaty provides that for the purpose of equitable distribution as between the Allies, the value of Annex deliveries shall be reckoned in the same manner as cash payments effected in the year, and the schedule of payments stipulates that the value of the deliveries received by each Power shall, within one month of the date of delivery, be paid over to the Reparation Commission, either in cash or in current coupons.

Further, the Treaty imposes upon the Reparation Commission not only the duty of fixing prices, but also of determining the capacity of Germany to deliver goods demanded by any of the Allies and, by implication, of deciding between the competing demands which are made upon that capacity of the Allies themselves.

148

The Wiesbaden Agreement provides for the delivery by a German company[1] to French 'sinistrés' of 'all plant and materials compatible with the productive capacity of Germany, her supply of raw materials and her domestic requirements', that is to say, of the articles and materials which can be demanded under Annex IV and Paragraph 19 of Annex II, which are, by the terms of the Agreement, in so far as France is concerned, virtually suspended, the obligations of Germany to deliver to France under the other Annexes remaining unaffected.

Any question as to the capacity of Germany to satisfy the requirement of France, and all questions of price, are to be settled by a Commission of three members, one French and one German, and a third selected by common agreement or nominated by the Swiss President.

The aggregate value of the deliveries to be made under the Agreement, and of the deliveries to be made under Annexes III, V, and VI (hereafter, for the sake of brevity, called the 'Annex deliveries') in the period expiring on 1 May 1926, is fixed at a maximum of 7 milliard gold marks.

In regard to the Annex deliveries the Agreement in no way modifies the Treaty provisions under which Germany is credited and France debited forthwith with the value, but special provisions, which are financially the essential part of the Agreement, are made for bringing to reparation account the value of the Agreement deliveries. These special provisions are designed to secure that Germany shall only be credited on reparation account at the time of delivery with a certain proportion of them, and that deliveries not thus accounted for, which may be called 'excess deliveries', shall be liquidated over a period of years beginning at the earliest on 1 May 1926. The provisions themselves are somewhat intricate, comprising, as they do, a series of interacting limitations, and they require some elucidation.

(1) In no case is credit to be given to Germany in any one year for Annex and Agreement deliveries together to an amount exceeding 1 milliard gold marks.

(2) In no case is credit to be given to Germany in any one year for more than 45 per cent of the value of the Agreement deliveries or for more than 35 per cent if the value of the Agreement deliveries exceeds 1 milliard gold marks.

---

[1] The arrangement under which a German private company is to be created to deal directly with the orders without the intervention of the French and German Governments is intended to obviate the delays which experience has shown to be inseparable from the employment of the present machinery. It does not appear to have any important bearing on the general financial situation, since the deliveries will clearly have to be financed by the German Government and will ultimately be paid for by means of a reparation credit in account with the German Government.

The effect of the above is to prescribe that 55 per cent (or, if the Agreement operates successfully, 65 per cent) of the value of the Agreement deliveries *as a minimum* will be the object of deferred payment by instalments. If the Agreement deliveries reached really high figures, the operation of the milliard limitation would make the carry-forward much more than 65 per cent.

The excess deliveries are to be liquidated with interest at 5 per cent per annum in 10 equal annual instalments as from 1 May 1926, subject to certain conditions:

(1) France shall in no case be debited in one year for Agreement deliveries with an amount which, when added to the value of her Annex deliveries in that year, would make her responsible for more than her share (52 per cent) of the total reparation payments made by Germany in that year.

(2) Agreement deliveries continue after 1 May 1926, with the same provisions for deferred payment. If in any year between May 1926 and May 1936 the amount (not exceeding 35 or 45 per cent) of the value of that year's Agreement deliveries to be credited to Germany, together with the annual instalment to repay the debt incurred in respect of the period ending 1 May 1926, exceeds 1 milliard, the excess is to be carried forward from year to year until a year is reached in which no such excess is created by the payment. But in no case shall the amount credited, even if it is less than 1 milliard gold marks, exceed the limit laid down by the preceding condition.

(3) Any balance with which Germany has not been credited on 1 May 1936 is to be credited to her with compound interest at 5 per cent in four half-yearly payments on 30 June and 31 December 1936 and 30 June and 31 December 1937. But, again, these half-yearly payments shall not be made if the effect of making them would be to exceed the limit laid down in Condition 1 above.

(4) Agreement deliveries continue indefinitely after 1 May 1936, with power, however, to Germany to arrest them whenever the execution of them would result in France owing more than 52 per cent of Germany's annual reparation payment in respect of Annex deliveries, deferred payments already matured, and the 35 or 45 per cent of current deliveries.

From the above it is to be noted that, while there is a limitation for the first five years of the amount of Agreement deliveries which can be demanded, there is:

(1) No point at which the right of France to demand these special deliveries automatically terminates.

(2) No final limitation upon the value of the deliveries which can be demanded by France during the lifetime of the Agreement.

(3) No definitely prescribed period within which France's debt to Germany and to the other partners in reparation shall be liquidated.

It remains necessary to draw attention to one subsidiary point of a financial character under the Schedule of Payments. Part of Germany's annual reparation liability consists of the payment of 26 per cent of the value of German exports in each period of twelve months, and part of the security for the payment consists of the proceeds of a levy of 25 per cent on the value of all German exports. The French Government has undertaken to support a request, to be submitted by the German Government to the Reparation Commission, for the inclusion in the exports which form the basis of these calculations of that part only of the value of the deliveries made under the Agreement which is credited to Germany and debited to France during any particular year.

If it can be assumed that any part of the special deliveries to be made under the Agreement would, in the absence of the Agreement, have been diverted to Germany's ordinary external trade, then the concession desired will have the effect of diminishing the annual payments made by Germany for the benefit of the Allies as a whole.

### 2. Decision of the Reparation Commission on 20 October 1921, after considering the Franco-German Agreement of 6 October 1921

The French Government, having submitted to the Reparation Commission in accordance with Paragraph 3 of the memorandum thereto attached the Agreement between the representatives of the French and German Governments signed at Wiesbaden on the 6th instant, the Commission has come to the following decision:

(1) It entirely approves the general principles underlying the Agreement whereby special arrangements are proposed for enabling Germany to liquidate the largest possible proportion of her reparation obligations in the form of goods and services, more especially with a view to the speedier restoration of the devastated regions.

(2) At the same time, it considers that the Agreement involves certain departures from the provisions of Part VIII of the Treaty of Versailles, notably Article 237, Paragraphs 12 and 19 of Annex II and Paragraph 5 of Annex IV.

(3) As the Commission has no power to authorise such departures, it decides to refer the question to the Governments represented on the Commission, with a copy of the Memorandum and its Annex, recommending a favourable examination of them.

(4) The Commission recommends that reasonable facilities for deferred

payment in respect of the exceptional volume which, if the arrangements are successful, the deliveries in kind to France are likely to assume during the next few years, should be accorded to France, subject to any safeguards which the Allied Governments may regard as necessary to protect their respective interests.

### 3. *Concluding recommendations of Sir John Bradbury's report to the British government (26 October 1921)*

The safeguards which are envisaged as necessary by my Italian and Belgian colleagues on the Reparation Commission and myself, and for which we presume that our respective Governments will desire to stipulate are:

(1) That a limit of time should be laid down after the expiration of which no new deferment of debit should be permitted and the liquidation of the existing deferred debits should commence to be made by regular annual instalments.

The precise length of this period should be determined upon an estimate of the time necessary to carry out the main work of reconstruction, regard being had to the time required by Germany to effect the necessary supplies. In view of the delays which are inevitable in regard to operations of the magnitude of those contemplated, the prescribed period might be reasonably somewhat longer than the four and a half years' initial period under the agreement, but it should not exceed seven years.

(2) That in no circumstances should the aggregate amount for which debit against France for the time being stands deferred be allowed to exceed a prescribed amount, say, 4 milliard gold marks.

(3) That a provision should be inserted for the payment by France to the general reparation account from time to time (within the limits of the deferred debits for the time being outstanding) of any amounts which may be necessary to secure that the other Allies shall receive their proper proportions of the amounts due from Germany under the schedule of payments.

Subject to the introduction of these safeguards, to which it would not appear that legitimate exception could be taken, the arrangements contemplated by the agreement may be expected to accelerate the solution of the Reparation problem on practical lines in a manner advantageous to France without prejudicing the interests of other Powers, and it is upon this ground that the Reparation Commission has unanimously recommended them for favourable examination by the Allied Governments.

If the Allied Governments approve the general scheme, subject to whatever safeguards they may decide to be necessary, there will remain certain subsidiary points for the Reparation Commission to consider—amongst other:

(1) The proposed omission of the excess deliveries from the index figure determining the annual liability under the Schedule of Payments, until such time as these deliveries are finally brought to account for reparation purposes.

(2) The special arrangements for substitution in respect of articles of which France is entitled to restitution by identity, involving in certain cases money payments; and

(3) The special arrangements in regard to the delivery of coal and the prices to be credited and debited, which in several particulars affect the interest of other Powers.

## 9. TABLES OF INTER-GOVERNMENTAL INDEBTEDNESS

### (A) Advances by the United States government to other governments (as in July 1921) (dollars)

| | Credits granted under Liberty Loan Acts[1] | Surplus war materials sale | Food relief | Grain Corporation | Interest[2] accrued and unpaid up to July 1921 | Total[2] obligations |
|---|---|---|---|---|---|---|
| Armenia | — | — | 8,028,412.15 | 3,931,505.34 | — | 11,959,917.49 |
| Austria | — | — | — | 24,055,708.92 | — | 24,055,708.92 |
| Belgium | 347,691,556.23 | 27,588,581.14 | — | — | 34,000,000 | 409,280,147.37 |
| Cuba | 9,025,500.00 | — | — | — | — | 9,025,500.00 |
| Czechoslovakia | 61,256,256.74 | 20,621,994.54 | 6,428,089.19 | 2,873,238.25 | 6,000,000 | 97,179,528.72 |
| Esthonia | — | 12,213,377.88 | 1,785,767.72 | — | — | 13,999,145.60 |
| Finland | — | — | 8,281,926.17 | — | — | 8,281,926.17 |
| France | 2,950,762,938.19 | 400,000,000.00 | — | — | 284,000,000 | 3,634,762,938.19 |
| Great Britain | 4,166,318,358.44 | — | — | — | 407,000,000 | 4,573,318,358.44 |
| Greece | 15,000,000.00 | — | — | — | — | 15,000,000.00 |
| Hungary | — | — | — | 1,685,835.61 | — | 1,685,835.61 |
| Italy | 1,648,034,050.90 | — | — | — | 161,000,000 | 1,809,034,050.90 |
| Latvia | — | 2,521,869.32 | 2,610,417.82 | — | — | 5,132,287.14 |
| Liberia | 26,000.00 | — | — | — | — | 26,000.00 |
| Lithuania | — | 4,159,491.96 | 822,136.07 | — | — | 4,981,628.03 |
| Poland | — | 59,636,320.25 | 51,671,749.36 | 24,353,590.97 | — | 135,661,660.58 |
| Roumania | 23,205,819.52 | 12,922,675.42 | — | — | 2,500,000 | 38,628,494.94 |
| Russia | 187,729,750.00 | 406,082.30 | 4,465,465.07 | — | 19,000,000 | 211,601,297.37 |
| Serbia | 26,175,139.22 | 24,978,020.99 | — | — | 3,500,000 | 54,653,160.21 |
| Totals | $9,435,225,329.24 | $565,048,413.80 | $84,093,963.55 | $56,899,879.09 | $943,500,000 | $11,084,767,585.68 |

[1] This is a *net* figure and allows for repayments made up to July 1921, of which the chief items are $78 million by France, and $111 million by Great Britain.

[2] The totals at the foot of these two columns include miscellaneous items for interest not entered in the particulars given in the columns themselves. A further sum of about $250 million will have accrued for interest by February 1922.

(B) *Advances by the British government to other governments*
(*as on 31 March 1921*)

| Allied governments[1] | £ | s | d | £ | s | d |
|---|---|---|---|---|---|---|
| France | 557,039,507 | 6 | 8 | | | |
| Russia | 561,402,234 | 18 | 5 | | | |
| Italy | 476,850,000 | 0 | 0 | | | |
| Belgium | 103,421,192 | 8 | 9 | | | |
| Serbia | 22,247,376 | 12 | 5 | | | |
| Montenegro | 204,755 | 19 | 9 | | | |
| Roumania | 21,393,662 | 2 | 8 | | | |
| Portugal | 18,575,000 | 0 | 0 | | | |
| Greece | 22,577,978 | 9 | 7 | | | |
| Belgian Congo | 3,550,300 | 0 | 0 | | | |
| | | | | 1,787,262,007 | 18 | 3 |
| Loans for relief | | | | | | |
| Austria | 8,605,134 | 9 | 9 | | | |
| Roumania | 1,294,726 | 0 | 8 | | | |
| Serbo-Croat–Slovene Kingdom | 1,839,167 | 3 | 7 | | | |
| Poland | 4,137,040 | 10 | 1 | | | |
| Czechoslovakia | 417,392 | 3 | 3 | | | |
| Esthonia | 241,681 | 14 | 2 | | | |
| Lithuania | 16,811 | 12 | 4 | | | |
| Latvia | 20,169 | 1 | 10 | | | |
| Hungary | 79,997 | 15 | 10 | | | |
| Armenia | 77,613 | 17 | 2 | | | |
| Inter-Allied Commission on the Danube | 6,868 | 17 | 6 | | | |
| | | | | 16,736,603 | 6 | 2 |
| Other loans (stores, etc.) | | | | | | |
| Czechoslovakia | 2,000,000 | 0 | 0 | | | |
| Armenia | 829,634 | 9 | 3 | | | |
| | | | | 2,829,634 | 9 | 3 |
| Total | | | | £1,806,828,245 | 13 | 8 |

[1] These accounts include interest, except in the case of Belgium and Serbia, from whom interest has not been charged, and in the case of Russia, where no interest has been entered up since January 1918.

## 10. THE CANNES MORATORIUM, 13 JANUARY 1922

At the end of the Cannes Conference the Reparation Commission issued the following communiqué:

The Reparation Commission decides to grant to the German Government a provisional postponement of the instalments due on 15 January and 15 February, 1922 (in so far as they are not covered by cash payments already made or which may be made, and by deliveries in kind and receipts under the Reparation Recovery Acts received or which may be received up to the respective due dates), subject to the following conditions:

(*a*) During the period of provisional postponement the German Government shall pay, in approved foreign currencies, the amount of 31 millions of gold marks every ten days, the first payment being upon 18 January 1922.

(*b*) The German Government shall, within a period of 15 days, submit to the Commission a scheme of budget and currency reform, with appropriate guarantees, as well as a complete programme of cash payments and deliveries in kind for the year 1922.

(*c*) The period of provisional postponement shall end as soon as the Commission or the Allied Governments have taken a decision with regard to the scheme and programme indicated in paragraph (*b*).

Except and so far as may be otherwise provided in this decision, the difference between the amounts actually paid during the period of the provisional postponement and the sums due during the same period under the Schedule of Payments shall become due and payable within 15 days from the date of the decision of the Reparation Commission or of the Allied Governments, as the case may be.

When the scheme and programme referred to above have been received by the Reparation Commission, they will be immediately transmitted by the Commission to the Allied Governments, who will thus be in a position either to deal with the matter themselves or to refer it back to the Commission to be dealt with by the latter.

# INDEX

Allied debts, 109 f., 118 f., 154
Armistice negotiations, 94, 95 f.
Army of occupation, expenses of, 54 *n*, 86 f.,
90, 123
Austria, 83, 122, 123

Balfour, A. J., 95 *n* 3
Baruch, 46 *n* 2, 68 *n* 1, 99, 100, 102, 103
*n* 1
Belgian priority, 86–7, 89–90, 122, 131
Reparation claims, 79, 127
Boulogne Conference, 11
Boyden, 71, 84
Bradbury, Sir John, 59, 61, 82 *n*, 83, 148
Brenier, 70, 75 *n* 3
Briand, 15, 16, 25–6, 44, 73
British Reparation Claims, 80, 136
Brockdorff-Rantzau, 17, 18
Brussels Conference (Experts), 13–14
Brussels Conference (League of Nations),
55
Brussels Conference (Premiers), 11
Bulgaria, 88, 122

Clemenceau, 54 *n* 2, 69, 96, 97
Coal, 28 ff., 48, 62–3
Cunliffe, Lord, 46, 100
Curzon, Lord, 36 *n*

D'Abernon, Lord, 19
Decisions of London, 61
Disarmament of Germany, 9–11
Dominion Prime Ministers' Conference,
89 *n* 1
Doumer, 71, 91
Dubois, 70–1, 73 *n*, 82 *n*
Dulles, John Foster, 101

East Prussia (plebiscite), 6
*Economic Consequences of the Peace*, 2, 24,
28, 32–3, 34 *n*, 46 *n* 1, 47 *n* 2, 68, 69,
73, 76, 80, 81 *n*, 93, 94 *n*, 107, 111
Elsas, Dr Moritz, 56, 57, 59 *n* 1
Exports, German, 50–2, 63, 106–7

Financial Agreement of Paris (August 1921),
87, 90–1
Foch, Marshal, 19, 20, 36, 95 *n* 3
Forgeot, 44 *n*

Fournier-Sarlovèze, 74 *n*
Frankfurt, Occupation of, 9, 36
French Reparation Claim, 69 ff., 75–9

George, Lloyd, 1, 10, 11, 13, 16, 18 ff., 25,
54 *n* 2, 78, 88 *n*, 2 89, 97, 100, 115
German budget, 52 f.
German counter-proposal (March 1921),
18–20
German counter-proposal (April 1921),
22 f., 139–41
German individual income, 55 f.
German property in United States, 50, 92
Gladstone, 3
Guarantees, Committee of, 43 f.

Haig, Sir Douglas, 95 *n*
Harding, President, 110
Heichen, Dr Arthur, 56
Helfferich, 57, 58
*History of the Peace Conference of Paris*,
95 *n* 2, 98 *n* 2, 103 *n* 1
House, Col., 95 *n* 3
Hughes, W. M., 100
Hungary, 123
Hymans, 97
Hythe Conference, 11

Invasion of Germany, 19, 20, 22
Italian Reparation Claims, 81, 137
Italy, 122

Kaiser, trial of, 8
Kapp, 'Putsch', 9
Klotz, 15, 36, 70, 71, 95, 97, 98

Lamont, J. W., 68 *n* 1, 104 *nn*
Lansburgh, Dr Albert, 56
Law, Bonar, 97
League of Nations, 6–7, 38–40, 121
Leipzig trials, 8
Léry, Raphaël-Georges, 76 *n*
Leygues, 13, 14
Lignite, 34 f.
London Conference I, 17, 21
London Conference II, 25
London Settlement, 41 f., 46, 47, 52, 54 *nn*,
83, 121, 143
London Ultimatum I, 18–19, 22, 138 f.

157